Free Pilgrim

— P I L G R I M —

To Charlie and Karen
May your lifelong
journey be filled
with joy

27/08/2016

Suite 300 - 990 Fort St
Victoria, BC, V8V 3K2
Canada

www.friesenpress.com

Copyright © 2016 by Pilgrim
First Edition — 2016

All rights reserved.

No part of this publication may be reproduced in any form, or by any means, electronic or mechanical, including photocopying, recording, or any information browsing, storage, or retrieval system, without permission in writing from FriesenPress.

ISBN
978-1-4602-8741-5 (Hardcover)
978-1-4602-8742-2 (Paperback)
978-1-4602-8743-9 (eBook)

1. *Travel*

Distributed to the trade by The Ingram Book Company

Table of Contents

A Short Note of Introduction	1
Steps of Paul	3
Nicolas of Bari	22
Lourdes	32
Fátima	45
Camino de Santiago	58
Cultural Pilgrimage	200
Solitude (Subiaco), Italy	276
The Holy City: Understanding the Past	308
The Road to Ancient Corinth	337
Journey to the New World (*Mundus Novus*)	354
New Life (to Be Born Again)	390
The Way (Spiritual Space)	413
Clash of Cultures	441
Resources and Further Reading	458
About the Author	461

*For my loving wife May "bersherte" and constant
companion with whom I share the joy -*

*For my understanding children Selena and
Nigel from their imperfect father-*

For all the kind souls who decide to walk with me despite our differences -

A Short Note of Introduction: Who am I?

I am still searching... but in the physical world, I am just an ordinary person smelling the roses, so to speak, and no longer wearing a tie or a wig and court band. I travel light and globe-trot around the world as a cultural pilgrim, trying to counter bigotry by sharing and enjoying stories in the constant search for an inner spiritual path. I was trained as a Barrister-at-Law at the Honourable Society of the Inner Temple England and was called to the Bar of England and Wales in 1966.

Barrister-at-Law of the Honourable Society of the Inner Temple England (1966).

I was Attorney-General of the State of Sabah, Malaysia (1976–1985), and I was a founding member and president (1986–1990) of the Sabah Golf and Country Club. The Central Bank Malaysia (Bank Negara) appointed me Chairman and Chief Executive of Sabah Bank (1987–1997) to restructure the bank, which eventually merged with Alliance Bank Malaysia. I initiated and was the founder and president (1991–1995) of the Council of the Justices of the Peace in Sabah, Malaysia.

I believe that dedication to a spiritual path will open up and provide a space in our otherwise busy, secular lives and allow for deep and profound personal transformation so we can receive the abundance of every gift beyond our expectations and imagination.

I like to encourage people to understand that there are really three persons in each and every one of us. I look in the mirror and see myself as the first person. Someone else would look at me and see the second person, because I am being read like the cover of a book. But there is really a third person in me, and my hope is you can see this third person. I always have hope—hope that there will be "willingness" in all of us—and my greatest hope is for all of us to be willing to accept Grace, which is freely given, to let the Holy Spirit fill the space of the third person in all of us.

Peace be with you,

Nicholas

Come and walk with me.

Steps of Paul

In the spring of 2009, I pack=ed and made preparation for my journey from Hagia Sophia in Constantinople (modern-day Istanbul) onto the grounds of Eastern Thrace, Lydia, Lycia, Phrygia, Pamphylia, Cappadocia, and Cilicia and all the way to Antioch (modern-day Antakya). Here is my story to relatives and friends in 2009.

Hagia Sophia is an architectural treasure with remarkable examples of Byzantine mosaics located in Constantinople (modern-day Istanbul, Turkey). It has stood for more than 1,500 years and is renowned in particular for its massive dome. It is considered the epitome of Byzantine architecture.

Inside Hagia Sophia, 2009. Christian and Islamic arts mingle in Hagia Sophia. Hagia Sophia was a great Christian cathedral (Greek Orthodox patriarchal basilica) until the mid-1400s. After the conquest of Constantinople by the Ottomans, Hagia Sophia became a mosque. It has since been opened as a museum (1935).

Journey to Turkey (2009)

I am not the world's greatest writer. I was gently nudged into producing this short article regarding my recent trip to Turkey, a land of biblical importance rich in history and fascinating culture. When I told people I was going to Turkey, they would invariably ask me, "Business or pleasure?" My answer would be "Neither". Neither did I want to sound like I was going to walk a journey of pilgrimage, because it wasn't really meant to be.

Travel agents have for many years been selling "the journeys of St. Paul" to eager Christian travellers. I have done enough research to know that it is not possible to follow the steps of St. Paul, let alone try to do any of his three journeys in these troubled times. Some places mentioned in Scripture no longer exist, or even if they do, those places can never be reached today by people like me because of political or security reasons.

A typical Roman amphitheatre, as seen in 2009.

There are also many insurmountable problems to be overcome in both transportation and communications. However, names mentioned in the Acts of the Apostles, such as Phrygia, Pamphylia, and Cappadocia, brought out the adventurer and vagabond in me. Would it be possible for me to still see places like Ephesus, Smyrna, Pergamum, Thyatira, Sardis, Philadelphia, and Laodicea in this age and time? I had the desire to visit Ephesus, where Paul had spent a considerable length of time, and perhaps from there try to get to Tarsus (his birthplace) and then go on to Antioch (modern-day Antakya), near the Syrian border.

The remains of the Temple of Artemis. The City of Ephesus prided itself on its designation "Temple Warden (*neokoros*) of Artemis" (Acts 19:35).

I wanted and decided to travel this journey on my own by bus. Organised tours are too restrictive and regimented for me. I like to explore. Tarsus and Antioch on the Orontes (unlike Ephesus) are not places of interest for most travellers. Thousands of tourists visit the world-famous Ephesus every year. The majority of them travel there from the cruise port of Kusadasi or go direct from Istanbul.

PILGRIM

Multitudes of visitors and pilgrims calling at Ephesus, as seen during my second journey there in 2014.

2014.

Everyone who visited Ephesus was affected in some way and came away with different feelings. My own feelings are reflected in the following poem I wrote to my relatives and friends:

> *Paul came to Ephesus trekking along a stony track;*
> *I arrived in an air-conditioned bus with pads for my back.*
> *Standing astride upon the mighty steps of Ephesus,*
> *I tried to visualize a journey so long ago from Tarsus.*
> *As I face the challenges of this, my journey, and yonder,*
> *I thank the good Lord for this opportunity to venture and ponder.*

Library of Celsus, 2009.

The Great Theatre of Ephesus where Paul used to preach, as we saw it in the spring of 2014. It was built into the slope of Mount Pion in the city centre and is reckoned to have accommodated more than 20,000 people.

A view of the Arcadian Way, as seen in 2009. The remains of Hellenistic and Roman Ephesus that can be seen today stand about 2 km from the site of the Temple of Artemis. Because of silting over the centuries, the city, which was a seaport during the New Testament time, now stands about 10 km inland. From the top of the amphitheatre, we could still discern the outline of the ancient harbour, which is now marshy wasteland at the end of the Arcadian Way.

A view from the Amphitheatre towards the Arcadian Way, as seen during my second journey to Ephesus in the spring of 2014.

A view to the Amphitheatre from the Arcadian Way in 2014. I noticed it had been better paved with granite slabs since my last visit in 2009.

The House of Mary, 2009. According to predominant Christian tradition, the Apostle John brought Mary to Ephesus after the Resurrection of Christ, and she lived out her days there. This idea is based mainly on the traditional belief that John came to Ephesus (Refer: St. John's Basilica of Ephesus) combined with John 19:26–27.

Archaeologists who have examined the building identified as the House of Mary believe most of the building dates from the 6th or 7th century, but its foundations are believed to be older: they probably date from the 1st century AD.

Pilgrims queuing in 2014 to enter the House of Mary, which has long been a place of pilgrimage for Christians.

A portrait of Blessed Anne Catherine Emmerich (1774–1824), a Roman Catholic nun who received a vision of the last abode of Mary.

I was in Turkey for almost a month and naturally have a lot of stories to tell besides describing kebabs, Turkish Delights, and baklava, but you don't want to listen to them. It is even less desirable for me to write about them in The Apostle. *There is, however, one incident (an unscheduled day trip) in my long journey that I wish to share with you and which I have already shared with my relatives and friends. I wrote about it in verse:*

A small step I took away from the Steps of Paul.
Stumbled I upon a sight I watched with awe.
There appeared before my eye the tomb of St. Nicholas,
He whom we knoweth well the night before Christmas.
St. Nicholas hath by temporal hand been commercialized
During the wintry months in more ways than he had realized.
Knoweth so few St. Nicholas was the Bishop of Myra
In an unknown little town I have come to admire.
When flowers in Myra I believe were in full bloom,
That it was from its nearby harbour, Paul set sail for Rome.

Museum (burial ground) of St. Nicolas in Myra.

From Myra I travelled back to Antalya, and from there I took an overnight bus to Cappadocia. In Cappadocia, I met a Zen Buddhist from Taiwan who related to me her own life experience and her faith.

(2009) Rock churches of Göreme.

(2009) Night bus from Antalya (a seaport not to be confused with Antakya) to Kayseri in Cappadocia.

Fresco of crosses inside one of the cave churches in Göreme (2009).

With a group of eight, we explored the underground city and the fascinating and indescribable cave churches. I was mesmerized by the beautiful fresco inside the caves painted so many years ago.

My journey has strengthened and deepened my own faith and belief. I believe in the Living God, and as a Christian, I continue to seek the Truth. I cannot treat what has been revealed to me lightly. I have touched holy ground. In my own way, I touched and felt the ground upon which Saul of Tarsus used to tread. I cannot cherry-pick the Truth he spoke.

(2009) St. Paul's Well, Tarsus.

Bus from Mersin (near Tarsus) to Antakya (Antioch).

At St. Paul's Well (2009).

Altar of St. Peter's Cave Church in Antioch (modern-day Antakya).

Façade of St. Peter's Cave Church (originally built by the Crusaders and rebuilt in the 19th century).

The throne chair in St. Peter's Cave Church.

I stood before the altar of St. Peter's Cave Church in Antioch and went back to the roots of Christianity. I try in my own way to know and understand what Christianity is all about. That's me, and as you can see, it is all "I" in this closing paragraph, but I wished you were there with me to change that "I" into "we". You would also have shared Antakya künefe (the most delightful and delicious dessert) with me.

PEACE

Nicholas

Antakya künefe.

Antakya Archaeological Museum.

My thought: The Crusaders built the façade of St. Peter's Cave Church during their rule of Antioch, 1098–1268. Today, two random Muslim friends took me (on their motor bike) to this church. There is hope…

My revelation: "A step away from the Steps of Paul…"

During my journey to Turkey in 2009, I was staying in a small hotel in Antalya. I had earlier booked for a day tour to some local attractions. At 5:00 a.m. there was a knock on my door. It was someone from the hotel reception, and he said, "Mr. Fung, you have a phone call." I was thinking, *Who could be calling me at this unearthly hour?* I went downstairs to answer the call, because I had no phone in my room. It was my travel agent, who told me that my tour for the day had been cancelled because there were only two English-speaking tourists. He asked whether I would mind joining a Russian tour group. He told me that the tour might interest me because it would be taking the group to the Museum of St. Nicolas. I had never heard of the Bishop of Myra (now revealed to me as St. Nick). I wrote to my family and friends a short poem about it afterwards, and the rest is mystery.

The fresco of St. Nick (revealed) in Myra.

Peace be with you,

Nicholas

> *"For I do not seek to understand in order to believe, but I believe in order to understand. For I believe this: unless I believe, I will not understand."*
>
> —Anselm of Canterbury

My journey continues...

Nicolas of Bari

St. Nicolas of Bari (Latin: *Sanctus Nicolaus*), 15 March 270–6 December 343, also called Nikolaos of Myra, was a historic Christian saint who was the Bishop of Myra (the modern-day Antalya Province on the Mediterranean coast of Turkey).

He is also known as Nikolaos the Wonder Worker because of the many miracles attributed to his intercession. In the year 2009 on my journey into Turkey (Steps of Paul), I first visited his tomb (museum) in Myra by coincidence or "by guidance of the Holy Spirit," as illuminated to me by a former pastor friend of mine. Some Italian sailors (believed to be Franciscan monks) moved the remains and relics of St. Nicolas from his tomb in Myra to Bari, Italy, in the year 1087.

Basilica San Nicolas in Bari, Italy.

Here is a poem I wrote about my visit to the tomb:

Five years in the making, this journey of mine,
From the day stumbled I upon a sight so fine
Within a cave with fresco and writing in Greek,
From which learned I the story of Saint Nick:
That long ago in a place we now called Demre,
Where from pilgrims took his remains in a hurry,
Transported the same to the city known as Bari,
Located at the heel of the graceful boot of Italy.

Now, my journey into Bari is one I like to share,
As I recall that once wrote I to those who cared:
A small step I took away from the Steps of Paul.
Stumbled I upon a sight I watched with awe.
There appeared before my eye the tomb of St. Nicholas,
He whom we knoweth well the night before Christmas.
St. Nicholas hath by temporal hand been commercialized
During the wintry months in more ways than he had realized.
Knoweth so few St. Nicholas was the Bishop of Myra,
In an unknown little town I have come to admire;
When flowers in Myra I believe were in full bloom,
It was from its nearby harbour Paul set sail for Rome.

The decorative ceiling of the Basilica.

In the spring of 2014, five years after my visit to the tomb (museum) of St. Nicolas in Myra, I was blessed with the opportunity of a pilgrimage to Bari, Italy, to pay respect to the Wonder Worker at his tomb. Although born and raised in the Lutheran tradition, I have learned to appreciate the Orthodox Christian's veneration of the relics of St. Nicholas. Pilgrimages to the basilica have increased exponentially, not only on his feast day but throughout the year.

A view of the faithful from the narthex.

The crypt under the basilica.

A crypt was completed by October 1089, and Pope Urban II laid the relics of St. Nicolas beneath the crypt's altar, consecrating a shrine that became one of medieval Europe's great centres for Christian pilgrimage. The present basilica over the crypt was completed in the middle of the 12th century. Although the basilica belongs to the Roman Catholic Church and is managed by the monks of the Dominican Order, it is an ecumenical centre.

The basilica is now an ecumenical centre.

A chapel for Orthodox liturgy.

In 1966 at one side of the crypt, an Orthodox chapel was established to provide for Orthodox liturgy. The ecumenical vision of the Dominican brothers sees St. Nicholas as everyone's saint, serving to bring together Christians of varying expressions from both East and West to worship God in unity.

The Tomb of St. Nicolas in the crypt underneath the church.

In spite of the crowd of people (with different tongues) in the crypt, there is relative quietness and at times even reverential silence as Christians of different denominations and countries pray in common spiritual unity.

Stone sarcophagus of St. Nick in Myra, 2009.

Peace be with you,

Nicholas

Lourdes

Lourdes is located in southern France in the foothills of the Pyrenees mountains. On 11 February 1858, a 14-year-old local girl, Bernadette Soubirous, claimed that a lady (the faithful believe her to be the Blessed Virgin Mary) appeared to her in the remote Grotto of Massabielle.

A distant view from Château Fort de Lourdes.

The lady appeared 18 times, and by 1859, thousands of pilgrims were visiting Lourdes. A statue of Our Lady of Lourdes was erected at the site in 1864. At the time of the apparitions, the grotto was on common land that was used by the villagers variously for pasturing animals, for collecting firewood, and as a garbage dump; it was considered to be unworthy.

The train station in Lourdes.

We arrived at Lourdes by high-speed train from Nice in the summer of 2007 and stayed at the Best Western Beausejour, just across from the train station. Lourdes is also served by Tarbes-Lourdes-Pyrénées Airport, although one can also fly into Pau Pyrénées Airport. The town's train station is served by both SNCF (France's national railway company) and TGV (*train à grande vitesse,* or high-speed) trains. The journey from Paris to Lourdes by train lasts five hours by TGV. Many pilgrims also arrive via bus service from France and Spain. Since we were in Nice the night before, it was very convenient for us to come with our Eurail pass.

Best Western Beausejour.

Délicieuse cuisine française.

I dislike the part of Lourdes with the neon-emblazoned gift shops overflowing with tawdry objects, souvenirs, and relics—"the bric-a-brac of piety", as some would call them. Lourdes has also been labelled by some as the "Disneyland of the Catholic Church". I can understand why it can be seen in this light, but I believe the Church has distanced itself from the commercialization. The many trinket stalls that we saw were privately owned, and the hawkers were forbidden inside the sanctuary.

Yearly from March to October, the Sanctuary of Our Lady of Lourdes is a place of mass pilgrimage from Europe and other parts of the world. Some believe the spring water from the grotto possesses healing properties.

The Basilica of Our Lady of the Rosary in the sanctuary is a place of mass pilgrimage from Europe and other parts of the world.

Stations of the Cross.

Witnessing the evening procession.

Since the apparitions, Lourdes has become one of the world's leading Catholic Marian shrines, and the number of visitors grows each year. According to the Wikipedia article on Lourdes, "an estimated 200 million people have visited the shrine since 1860, and the Roman Cathedral Church has officially recognized 69 healings considered miraculous. Cures are examined using Church criteria for authenticity and authentic miracle healing with no physical or psychological basis other than the healing power of the water."

A view from the Basilica of Our Lady of the Immaculate Conception of Lourdes.

The Grotto of Massabielle, in Lourdes.

Although born and raised in the Lutheran tradition, I have learned (and appreciate) that private revelations do not form part of the deposit of faith of the Catholic Church. The members of the Church are not bound to believe in any of them. However, as a matter of prudence, assent would normally be expected of a Catholic based on the discernment of the Church and its judgment that an apparition is worthy of belief.

Mass in Lourdes Basilica Notre Dame.

The procession of the faithful in Lourdes, as seen through the lens of my camera in 2008. From March to October, the Sanctuary of Our Lady of Lourdes is a place of mass pilgrimage from Europe and many other parts of the world.

Peace be with you,

Nicholas

Just a thought: God uses ordinary people in extraordinary ways. The Apostles were uneducated and had no formal theological training before they met Jesus. Jesus called them to follow him. They walked with Jesus for three years, day and night, watching him perform miracles and teaching them personally as he taught others. And the Great Commission continues...

Fátima

Fátima is a civil parish in the municipality of Ourém, Portugal. On 17 October 2013, we arrived at Caxarias station (just outside Fátima) from Porto by train. We had earlier travelled to Porto by coach from Santiago de Compostela, Spain (after our journey on the Camino de Santiago). There are also coaches from Porto (Batalha Bus Station) to Fátima by Rede-Expressos about once every two hours. Very few pilgrims/visitors disembarked with us at Caxarias station, as most passengers were on their way from Porto to Lisbon. Most pilgrims/visitors to Fátima come by way of train or coach from Lisbon.

At Caxarias station, we asked (with great difficulty) for information regarding public transport into Fátima but were informed that buses do not run at this time of the year. We then took a short taxi ride into town and checked into Hotel Anjo de Portugal (a four-star facility at US $49 a night because it was the off-season). Even though it was supposed to be the off-season in Fátima, we were still able to witness many events.

Looking down to the central plaza at the Shrine of Our Lady of Fátima.

The Basilica of Our Lady of Fátima.

The history of Fátima is associated with three Portuguese shepherd children, Lucia dos Santos, Jacinta Marto, and Francisco Marto, who were young and without much education. It was reported that while they were watching their sheep, they witnessed the apparition of a lady dressed in white. The lady later was referred to as (and believed by faithful to be) "Our Lady of the Rosary". She visited the children on the 13th day of each month from May to October 1917. The last apparition occurred on 13 October 1917 on the day of the "Miracle of the Sun".

Currently, pilgrimage to the site goes on year-round. The principal pilgrimage festivals take place on the 13th day of each month from May to October, on the anniversaries of the original appearances. The largest crowds gather on 13 May and 13 October, when it is reported that up to a million pilgrims attend to pray and witness processions of the statue of Our Lady of Fátima both during the day and at night by the light of tens of thousands of candles.

The Chapel of Apparitions.

During our visit, we witnessed the procession of the faithful in an atmosphere of extremely passionate religious devotion, with some pilgrims crawling on their knees towards the shrine. Hundreds prayed at the shrine both during the day and also at night. Groups of non-Catholic Christians (including representatives of the Orthodox Churches) had also come with the intention of asking for Church unity. Many Anglican priests accompanied by their bishop had held spiritual retreats in one of the houses there. Other personalities who are not Catholic, such as the Dalai Lama and the President of the Republic of India, had also visited Fátima. The intention of peace is universal.

Witnessing the procession.

The procession.

The procession.

Some devoted pilgrims crawled on their knees at the Marian shrine of Fátima in central Portugal on 20 October 2013. Thousands of pilgrims visit the shrine of the apparitions of Mary to three shepherd children. Lucia dos Santos and her cousins, Francisco and Jacinta Marto, received the first of several visions of Mary on 13 May 1917.

Visiting the sanctuary of Fátima is an uplifting experience for people of all faiths. I visited both the basilica and the newer church.

The basilica as we saw it at night in October 2013.

A view from the narthex of the basilica.

Fátima Sanctuary the shepherds' tombs (October 2013).

A short distance from the sanctuary of Our Lady of Fátima lies Aljustrel, where some of the apparitions took place. We followed the simple stone path that was constructed in the middle of the rural environment where the three shepherd children used to put their sheep to pasture. The path is punctuated by several small chapels that depict the Stations of the Cross; they were built from the donations of Hungarian refugees after the Second World War.

Procession of the devotees at the Stations of the Cross.

The Fourteenth Station: Jesus is laid in the tomb.

A statue of Pope John Paul II. Pope John Paul II credited Our Lady of Fátima with saving his life following the assassination attempt on Wednesday, May 13, the Feast of Our Lady of Fátima, in 1981. He followed in the footsteps of Paul VI on May 12, 1987 to express his gratitude to the Virgin Mary. The following day, John Paul II renewed the consecration of Pius XII to the Immaculate Heart of the Virgin.

In a town not far from the plaza, there is a Chinese restaurant where we feasted, as we had been deprived of the oriental cuisine since we had left the town of Santiago de Compostela (at the end of our pilgrimage on the Camino de Santiago).

Peace be with you,

Nicholas

Camino de Santiago

This particular *Camino* (path or way), Camino Francés, leads from the small village of Saint-Jean-Pied-de-Port in southern France to the ancient city of Santiago de Compostela in Galicia, Spain. This ancient path, which stretches over a distance of 800 kilometres, has been changing and transforming lives over the centuries and is indeed the most popular Christian pilgrimage route in the world. It was proclaimed the Council of Europe's first Cultural Route in 1987 and was inscribed as a World Heritage Site by UNESCO (the United Nations Educational, Scientific and Cultural Organization) in 1993.

Saint-Jean-Pied-de-Port.

My reason for publishing this blog is the hope that it will motivate viewers who are interested and have intended or intend to take this journey. As for me, the inspiration, teachings, and lessons derived from this pilgrimage will last a lifetime.

I had been training for this since the summer of 2012, and by August 2013, I was ready for the challenge to trek the 800 km, with my backpack weighing about 7.5 kg. I started out on 25 August 2013 after spending some time in the beautiful French village of Saint-Jean-Pied-de-Port (having arrived there by train from Charles de Gaulle Terminal two days before).

Taking my first step at Saint-Jean-Pied-de-Port.

I trekked over the Pyrenees and across four regions of northern Spain (cornfields, vineyards, chestnut trees, and bare muddy or rocky grounds), interacting with many people of different cultures from around the world. After having taken advice at the beginning of my journey, I had decided to pre-book my accommodations from the town of Sarria (a very popular starting point for the last stage of Camino Francés) onwards to Santiago. The weight on my back was from then on reduced to that of a day-pack. Symbolically, my burden was also lightened. It took me altogether 52 days (40 walking days) to complete this physical and spiritual journey, whereas some can manage to finish it in 33.

There are two ways to cross over the Pyrenees from Saint-Jean-Pied-de-Port, France, into Roncesvalles, Spain. My desire was not to walk the Route de Napoleon because I was not an experienced hiker. I decided to take the Way of St. James through Valcarlos instead. I am given to understand that we do not choose life, but to live it we need to make choices.

The beginning, 25 August 2013.

This strenuous route takes us through the woods, up and down steep hills and valleys, away from the dangerous N-135.

(25 August 2013) Beautiful view of the countryside and rolling hills along our way to Valcarlos.

It was drizzling as we were trekking through the woods up the Pyrenees. These hazel and beech woods (and further up, pine trees) provided us with reasonable cover from the wind and also would have provided shade on the way, had the hot summer sun appeared.

(26 August 2013) After spending our first night in Valcarlos, we got ready for the journey into Roncesvalle.

(26 August 2013) We were on our own and at our own walking speed, taking in the scenic beauty of the countryside.

(26 August 2013) Puerto de Ibañeta, altitude 1,055 metres, Pyrenees: We were grateful for the rain ponchos we packed. Despite the heavy downpour (perhaps our test on the start of this journey), we were full of joy.

In Basque country (Navarre) on the second day, we were being tested and had to cross the Pyrenees in miserable conditions, because the rain in Spain does not fall mainly on the plain... but we felt the joy!

(26 August 2013) On this day, our view from high above the Pyrenees.

We met a young couple from Brazil who took our photo at Puerto de Ibañeta. They brought with them their bicycles and with limited time were hoping to finish the Camino Francés on their bikes, in 12 days.

A young couple from Brazil.

(26 August 2013) We arrived at Roncesvalles after an arduous and strenuous hike over the Pyrenees and were ready for a beer at La Posada.

(27 August 2013) On the way to Zubiri after passing through the Navarese village of Burguete, where Ernest Hemingway used to stay.

Walked 22.5 km with some very rough sections leading down to Zubiri. However, on this day, we were walking in glorious Spanish sunshine.

(28 August 2013) Early pilgrims starting out from Zubiri.

(28 August 2013) Soon to arrive at Pamplona, famous worldwide for the San Fermín running of the bulls festival held in July.

(29 August 2013) Cathedral of Santa María, Pamplona. We stayed an extra day in Pamplona in order to visit the Church of St. Nicolas and the Cathedral of Santa María (we had the rare opportunity to watch and listen to the organ being tuned and played)... with extra time to walk the *calle Estafeta* (the bull run).

I got a taste of the "bull run" culture.

Sunflower bed outside Pamplona.

(30 August 2013) Trekking up to the summit of Alto del Perdón, 11.4 km from Pamplona.

Monumento al peregrino at Alto del Perdón is an iconic sculpture dedicated to all the pilgrims who walk the Camino de Santiago. The long metal sculpture depict pilgrims on foot as well as some on horseback reflecting the historical and eternal nature of the walk: "where the path of the wind crosses that of the stars". It is one of the great landmarks of the Camino.

(30 August 2013) Approaching Cirauqui. Today we struggled for 24.1 km up and over the windy hills and then down to the plain and got roasted by the Spanish summer sun in the process.

(30 August 2013) Puente La Reina (bridge of the queen) was named in honour of Doña Mayor, wife of Sancho III, who commanded this Romanesque bridge to be built to support the increasing number of pilgrims. We relaxed in the town of Puente la Reina, visiting Iglesias Santiago (Church of Saint James, of Romanesque origin) and the Church of the Crucifix... with bonus time to watch a movie crew filming on the bridge.

(1 September 2013) Puente La Reina to Estella.

2 September 2013.

(2 September 2013) Pilgrims queuing up for the wine. Along the Camino Francés, the winery Bodegas Irache has a wine fountain on the wall (just outside the town of Estella) so that pilgrims can serve themselves a free glass of wine to help spur them on their way.

(2 September 2013) Time for lunch under a tree—the only shade in the hot sun along a 5 km stretch from Cruce to Los Arcos after we took our coffee break in the village of Villamayor de Monjardín.

(2 September 2013) Night scene of Los Arcos.

A crossroads town between Estella and Logroño.

(3 September 2013) The hungriest pilgrim was the first one to enter the restaurant for the pilgrim dinner...

the place was quickly filled.

(3 September 2013) Water fountain by Iglesia de Santa Maria with a recessed doorway in Viana.

(4 September 2013) Cathedral of Logroño.

A typical pilgrim dinner menu showing selections. The dinner comes with dessert, a bottle of water, and a bottle of wine gratis.

(5 September 2013) Logroño... just one for nostalgia.

(5 September 2013) We took an extra day of rest in Logroño to rejuvenate our weary bodies.

(6 September 2013) Daybreak on the way from Logroño to Navarrete.

(6 September 2013) Pilgrims approaching Navarrete with discourse on the meaning of the bull statue on the hill in front of us.

(6 September 2013) Passing through many vineyards on the way to Navarrete.

(7 September 2013) On the way to Nájera with a threatening overcast sky that soon cleared up for us to have lunch at the rest area.

On 7 September 2013.

This "hive" is for inclement weather, I suppose.

(7 September 2013) Nájera, a historic town with strong connections with the Camino de Santiago, was in the kingdom of Navarre in the 11th and 12th centuries.

(8 September 2013) To Santo Domingo de la Calzada.

(9 September 2013) A view of the Church of Santo Domingo at a distance behind me as we continue our journey at the break of dawn.

Santo Domingo de la Calzada owes its inspiration to Saint Dominic (Spanish: *Santo Domingo*). St. Dominic (1170–1221) was a Spanish priest and founder of the Dominican Order. He effectively dedicated part of his life to improving the route for pilgrims by building many of the bridges we walked over. This was in the 12th century, so the bridges have since been rebuilt many times, but his spirit is alive.

(9 September 2013) With fellow pilgrims from Ireland.

(9 September 2013) Small world... met a university student, Eve, from France who had recently spent some time in Kota Kinabalu Sabah with a family we know.

(9 September 2013) Showing a modern-day pilgrim from San Francisco how to use WhatsApp to communicate with her son who was studying in Simon Fraser University (SFU).

(10 September 2013) Near Villafranca de Montes de Oca.

10 September 2013.

(10 September 2013) A view from our room in Hotel San Antón Abad in Villafranca Montes de Oca.

(11 September 2013) The 13th-century Burgos Cathedral, essentially Gothic, has been embellished by master architects and builders down through the centuries.

Inside the Burgos Cathedral, we saw a unique and magnificent collection of works of art and artefacts, including paintings, carvings, choir stalls, and stained-glass windows. This morning, we entered the cathedral by the evocative south door and even though the transept crossing was relatively crowded we were not distracted but were immediately mesmerised by the wealth of art treasures and artefacts . It was very noisy outside the Cathedral but we eventually found peace and quiet in the Iglesia de San Nicolás next to the cathedral while avoiding the maddening crowd watching the closing of a bicycle race.

We entered through the south door, passing many treasures and crossing the transept to the lovely Renaissance Golden Staircase.

The tranquillity inside the Burgos Cathedral and Iglesia Nicolás was contrasted by the noisy finish of Stage 16 of the Vuelta a España (bicycle tour) on Wednesday, 11 September 2013 (Calahorra–Burgos, 189 kilometres).

The winding up of Stage 16 of the Vuelta a España (bicycle tour) 2013 in Burgo.

(12 September 2013) Who is counting?

A serene scene of sheep grazing on the ground of Meseta (where there is no shade to protect pilgrims from the sun) as we were being ferried after seeking dispensation.

A view of the Iglesia de San Pedro from our hostel, San Pedro Frómista, on the evening of 13 September 2013.

(14 September 2013) An early start for "free pilgrim".

Iglesia de San Martín de Tours, a church built in the 11th century in Romanesque style, in Frómista, Palencia.

(14 September 2013) A comforting sight at the break of dawn.

(14 September 2013) Coffee break on the way from Frómista to Carrión de los Condes.

(14 September 2013) St. Francis of Assisi museum.

(14 September 2013) Pilgrims who had to spend the night in the open near the village of Carrión de los Condes.

(15 September 2013) Early pilgrims on the way to Calzadilla de la Cueza.

(15 September 2013) "Public Convenience"? We walked on the Via Aquitania (a paved Roman road with little shade) for about 17.25 km and decided to stay in a private *albergue* at Calzadilla de la Cueza...

(15 September 2013) Some enterprising soul putting up a breakfast stand for pilgrims on a stretch of 11.4 km without facilities. What you see is what you get...

(15 September 2013) "Energy food" at Calzadilla de la Cueza.

(15 September 2013) Friendly and hospitable folk not just pointing but walking with us and showing us the way to the village parish church.

(16 September 2013) Our early morning long shadows preceding us on the way to Terradillos de los Templarios.

(16 September 2013) Terradillos de los Templarios, formerly a stronghold of the Knights Templar. It is the halfway point between Saint-Jean-Pied-de-Port and Santiago de Compostela.

(16 September 2013) Taking a rest in the shade on the way to Moratinos.

(17 September 2013) Early pilgrims leaving Moratinos.

(17 September 2013) Pilgrims taking a rest at the peaceful village linked to the Templars San Nicolás del Real Camino with the parish church Iglesia de San Nicolás, which was under restoration at the time we were there.

(17 September 2013) The Ermita Virgen del Puente brought me across to an unpretentious sanctuary (the original hospice long gone) with a 12th-century Romanesque foundation.

(17 September 2013) Pilgrims on the way to Sahagún.

We passed through another peaceful village (San Nicolás del Real Camino) linked to the Templar Order and then proceeded to Sahagún to see what (little) remains of the famous abbey of San Benito, which was founded in the 10th century and rose to become one of the most important Benedictine monasteries in Spain.

(17 September 2013) Evening walk to Arco de San Benito, Sahagún.

(18 September 2013) Leaving Sahagún after a restful night at Domus Viatoris. Leaving Arco de San Benito in the early morn, we continued our Camino for El Burgo Ranero, passing Puente Canto, a historic stone bridge.

Puente Canto, a historic bridge that was originally Romanesque but was reconstructed in the 11th and 16th centuries with strong arches, which have stood the test of time.

(18 September 2013)
Staying and enjoy a beer at Hostal El Peregrino in El Burgo Ranero.

(19 September 2013) Sunrise at El Burgo Ranero.

(19 September 2013) We took the Real Camino Francés with modern *senda* on the way from El Burgo Ranero to Mansilla de las Mulas.

Realizing that we would be unable to travel like Emperor Augustus on the Roman road from El Burgo Ranero to León, we continued on the Camino via Mansilla de las Mulas and took refuge there for the night after walking 19.1 kilometres.

(19 September 2013) Trying very hard to understand.

(20 September 2013) It is recommended that pilgrims take a bus for the short stretch into the city of León because of the dangerous road traffic along the route that pilgrims have to compete with!

León—a former Roman garrison and base for its seventh legion.

The Gothic splendour of León Cathedral, or Pulchra Leonina, which towered above my head. The cathedral is an imposing presence bristling with spires and strongly built buttresses.

(20 September 2013) I walked into the cathedral with awe, craning my neck to look at the tapestry of lights flowing from rows of magnificent luminous stained-glass windows and down to the floor.

(20 September 2013) We spent two days in León—even though we could have spent days there and not been able to see half of it—and had the opportunity to watch cultural dances at the Plaza at night.

(22 September 2013) My thoughts were tinged with sadness in leaving León. We looked for the embedded Camino shells as we went on our way.

I was rewarded with this delicious *pulpo* (octopus) at a restaurant near Hotel Villapaloma where we stayed for the night, just at the outskirts of La Virgen del Camino.

(23 September 2013) Like most pilgrims, we took the pilgrim's alternative route via Valverde to Villadangos del Páramo.

After we had spent some time in the sanctuary of Virgen del Camino, another beautiful sunrise greeted us this morning. In search of accommodation, we will enter the village of Villadangos del Páramo (where we hope to get a glimpse of the statue of Santiago Matamoros) instead of the more popular Villar de Mazarife.

A church building that has long been abandoned.

(23 September 2013) We were the early pilgrims at the breakfast joint at Valverde, but speedy young pilgrims soon caught up with us.

The parish church Iglesia de Santiago, which is still being used; however, it was closed for service at the time we arrived in Villadangos del Páramo.

(23 September 2013) The parish church Iglesia de Santiago in Villadangos del Páramo, an old town of Roman origin.

The statute of Santiago Matamoros is seen leaping out towards us.

From Iglesia de Santiago (where the statue of Santiago Matamoros leaped out towards us), the Camino continued on a path adjacent to N-120. This was our noisiest day on the Camino. However, we managed to find relative peace and joy in casual conversation (in broken Spanish supplemented by sign language) with some folks working in their fields.

(24 September 2013) Learning and giving a helping hand.

(24 September 2013) Cornfields as far as our eyes could see.

(24 September 2013) I am lost for words and have no comment for this photo.

(24 September 2013) One of the longest and most well-preserved medieval bridges—a landmark on the Camino.

(24 September 2013) Our dinner at Hospital de Órbigo. I didn't think it was from Rio Órbigo.

(25 September 2013) Too early for me to tell what this is in the light of dawn.

Today the Camino took us once again to the serenity and peacefulness of the countryside and further into the beautiful city of Astorga, where we welcome the modern facilities in the midst of its ancient splendour.

Why does it remind me of another place in another country?

(25 September 2013) By now, I was getting used to seeing this sort of thing.

Enjoying some Spanish music before entering Astorga.

(25 September 2013) The city of Astorga is in the distance.

In Astorga, we felt the passing of the centuries and were enthralled by the evolution of religious architecture. The Astorga Cathedral (*Catedral de Santa María*) took centuries to build, with construction beginning in in 1471; it was completed only in the 18th century. Antoní Gaudí's Bishop's Palace (with its Baroque main façade) offers another good example of this architectural evolution.

We entered Astorga being greeted by the Cathedral of Santa Maria standing majestically over the square (*Plaza de la Catedral*) and by the *Episcopal Palacio* (Bishop's Palace), with its turrets soaring towards heaven.

Stained-glass windows in the *Episcopal Palacio*.

The Renaissance altarpiece with a Romanesque statue of *Virgen de la Majestad*.

(27 September 2013) We depart Astorga after spending two nights there—and with me still looking and pointing at magnificent buildings with admiration.

A hermitage welcoming pilgrims from all over the world.

We left Astorga on a cool, sunny morning, but soon the weather began to change (the first rain we experienced since the Pyrenees), making it necessary for us to seek shelter in one of the villages (Castrillo de los Polvazares) somewhere in the west of the Province of León.

(28 September 2013) We spent the night in Castrillo de los Polvazares.

We woke up at 6:30 a.m.—perhaps we were awakened by the rain. We debated and decided to proceed with our journey despite the miserable conditions. This early morning, we were tested in the pouring rain and felt forsaken and "lost". After we had walked perhaps less than 200 metres, a small car stopped in front of us on the cobblestone road. The driver wound down his window and spoke to us, but we could not comprehend. All we could deduce from his waving hand was a sign of "no". Since he sensed no comprehension on our part, he got out of his car (despite the rain), pointed in the direction of our path, and waved that "no" sign again to us and by another gesture encouraged us to enter his vehicle. We looked at each other, and my intuition told me he could be trusted to give us a ride. He took us for about 10 kilometres on a slightly different route to the nearest village. I offered to pay him, which he flatly refused. Until today, we have not the faintest idea why this happened. All we know is that it is most unusual for a Spanish man to be up at that hour.

(28 September 2013) Suddenly an "angel" appeared at the break of dawn to give us encouragement. He advised us not to proceed further and offered to take us to the next village to join other pilgrims for hot tea.

(28 September 2013) Santa Catalina de Somoza, where our "angel" took us to and where we had hot tea with fellow pilgrims.

(28 September 2013) Continuing on our journey after being rescued by our "angel".

(28 September 2013) Iglesia de Santa María. It is believed that the Knights Templar, who were here the 12th century to protect pilgrims, built this church.

(28 September 2013) "Lord... be our consolation during rejection, and the power of our intention, so that under your guidance, safely and unhurt, we may reach the end of our pilgrimage."—Pilgrimage prayer

(28 September 2013) Iglesia de Santa María, where we were blessed with the opportunity to attend a vesper service with Gregorian chants conducted by Benedictine monks from Bavaria. Photography was not actually allowed during service, but I managed to sneak in one picture (with reverence) for remembrance.

(29 September 2013)

The fleece came out from our backpacks for the first time this early Sunday morning at 9°C (felt like 6°). By midday, we left behind our beloved scallop shells at *Cruz de Ferro* (Iron Cross), a humble monument marking a majestic spot on Puerta Irago at 1,504 metres above sea level—the highest point on our Camino. We added these tokens of love and blessing to an enormous pile that bears witness to the collective journey of ours and the thousands of pilgrims who have (for centuries) gone before us.

(29 September 2013) Cruz de Ferro.

(29 September 2013) Manjarín, a little mountain refuge (with misty surroundings and atmosphere) where we took a break at the invitation of the aroma of coffee.

(29 September 2013) Arriving at El Acebo, a small mountain village with one street and an enterprising young couple from Barcelona who runs a small hotel and a restaurant.

(29 September 2013) Evening with our hosts, who cooked us a delicious dinner and made sumptuous sandwiches for us for the following day.

(30 September 2013) An early start for Molinaseca from the village of El Acebo.

(30 September 2013) On the way to Molinaseca (onward to Ponferrada) with one of the most scenic views on our Camino.

(30 September 2013) A Roman bridge that took me over to the delightful village of Molinaseca. The Church of St. Nicolas is on the rise.

We were able to view the displays of replicas of Templar manuscripts and other religious texts in the Templum Libri (Temple of Books).

(30 September 2013) We arrived at Ponferrada. The magnificent 12th-century Castillo Templario had recently reopened after extensive renovations.

(30 September 2013) After walking on the most gruesome section of the Camino (but compensated by the beautiful countryside and scenery), we arrived in Ponferrada and spent two nights in the Templar Hotel.

(2 October 2013) We saw this on the way to Cacabelos.

(2 October 2013) Hospitality shown by the farmers: they gave us grapes to quench our thirst and hunger.

(2 October 2013) We spent the night at Hostal Santa María in town of Cacabelos, which was an important medieval pilgrim stop with five hospices founded for the care of pilgrims on the way.

(3 October 2013) The river flows through.

(3 October 2013) An old olive press.

(3 October 2013) This donkey cried when we left. May told me to go back to talk to him. After I explained to him that we had to be on our way to Santiago de Compostela, he let us leave quietly.

(3 October 2013) Entering Villafranca del Bierzo, where we spent two nights.

(4 October 2013) The Church of St. Nicholas, which now is the Convent of the Padres Paúles.

(4 October 2013) This delightful town began to develop in this idyllic spot along the Camino Francés in the 11th century.

(3 October 2013) An evening at the Plaza Mayor with café tables spilling out into the square.

(5 October 2013) Before daybreak, we began our challenging and strenuous walk up the mountain via Trabadelo towards Vega de Valcarce.

(5 October 2013) High above the clouds.

(5 October 2013) The sun has come through, and we are now descending into the village of Vega de Valcarce.

(5 October 2013) At Vega de Valcarce, we were rewarded with these most delicious ribs for our pilgrims' dinner.

(6 October 2013) Some choose to ride horses up the most taxing and strenuous part of the Camino towards O'Cebreiro. I wanted to try it too, but the horses had all been taken...

(6 October 2013)... so I had to re-energize myself with chocolate bars again on the way up.

(6 October 2013) The picture tells the story of the difficult terrain on and up to O'Cebreiro in Galicia.

Today (6 October 2013) we leave the Castile-León to enter Galicia.

Iglesia de Santa María la Real de O'Cebreiro, one of the earliest buildings on the Camino with part dating from the 9th century.

The 12th-century statue *Santa María la Real* is displayed along with the chalice and paten connected with the miracle of Santo Milagro in the O'Cebreiro iglesia.

(7 October 2013) Leaving O'Cebreiro for Triacastela.

The weather in Galicia is unpredictable. The mountain is the first to be hit by the wind coming in from the Atlantic, so immediate changes in weather conditions, with frequent rain and thunderstorms, can be expected.

Approximately 133 km to Santiago and 18.5 km to Sarria.

(8 October 2013) And then we had bright sunshine.

(8 October 2013) And suddenly it became so foggy...

8 October 2013.

Sarria is the popular starting point of the last stage (115 km) for many who have limited time but are anxious to pick up a *Compostela*, a certificate showing that they have completed the pilgrimage. Starting from here, pilgrims can cover the requisite 100 km to the Cathedral in Santiago de Compostela. I had earlier decided to have our accommodations pre-booked and our backpacks transferred daily from this town onwards towards Santiago. The weight on my back was reduced to that of a day-pack. Symbolically, my burden was also lightened.

(9 October 2013) The evocative mural on the main street, Rúa Maior, in Sarria.

(9 October 2013). We decided to spend two days in Sarria to absorb the Galician culture...

(9 October 2013) ... and to enjoy the delicious calamari done the Galician way.

(9 October 2013) Evening in 13th-century church O Salvador, located on Rúa Maior in Sarria.

(10 October 2013) The former monastery is now being used as a school.

(10 October 2013) Pilgrims taking a break for morning coffee.

(10 October 2013) The modern bridge over the deep Miño River basin takes pilgrims from Vilachá into Portomarín. The original Roman bridge joined the northern district of San Nicolás (headquarters of the Knights of St. John) with the southern district of San Pedro (with links to the Knights of Santiago).

(10 October 2013) The austere 12th-century church of St. Nicholas, which was painstakingly reconstructed from its original site, is now submerged in the reservoir at Portomarín.

The altar of the 12th-century church of St. Nicholas at Portomarín.

(11 October 2013) The volunteer caretaker showing us around the church and trying to explain to us about the significance of relics and artefacts.

(11 October 2013) Signing the visitor book and penning an acknowledgment of thanks.

A detour to Vilar de Donas gave us the rare opportunity to enter the Church of El Salvador to view the unique effigies of the knights, frescoes, many artefacts, and treasures. A learned volunteer caretaker (a retired electrical engineer in his 80s) gave us a very instructive tour, for which we were very grateful indeed.

(11 October 2013) These effigies somehow reminded me of those in the Temple Church (of The Honourable Society of the Inner Temple) in which I had spent considerable time when I was a law student.

(11 October 2013) The farmer demonstrated how the peppers can be eaten straight from the plant raw...

(11 October 2013)... Thanks, but I prefer them fried and sprinkled with a bit of olive oil and salt to go with my burger and beer.

(12 October 2013) Trying very hard to understand this piece of art.

(12 October 2013) The stone cross, *Crucero do Melide*, reputed to be the oldest cross in Galicia—Christ in majesty facing us and Christ crucified in reverse.

13 October 2013.

Delightful Galician cuisine and beer.

Only 50 km to go...

(14 October 2013) Admiring a statue of the Knight Templar.

In conformity with popular culture, I had forgotten that the Order of the Knights Templar was originally founded around 1118 by Hugh de Payens (c. 1070–1136) to protect early Christian pilgrims travelling to the Holy Land. Their legacy in England includes the Temple Church (once the English Templars' headquarters) and the Honourable Societies of the Inner and Middle Temple, where barristers-at-law are trained.

14 October 2013.

I entered the city of St. James (Santiago de Compostela) with these thoughts: I arrived at the end of this pilgrimage with the realization that I had recently fallen when I preferred to remember only the ills of some but chose to inter the good of so many with their bones. Faith is personal and important to me. Without it, (my) life would be utterly meaningless—without depth and unquestionably poorer—despite all the wonderful earthly things I have been blessed with and for which I am thankful. My journey continues with the hope for more encouragement and the opportunity to share the Good News and God's abundance.

The Cathedral.

Pilgrim Mass (Ecumenical).

The *Compostela* with my name in Latin.

Peace be with you,

Nicholas

Just a thought: Dedication to a spiritual path will open up and provide a space in our busy, secular lives and allow for deep and profound personal change and transformation so we can receive the abundance of every gift. Walk with me as I continue with my journey in search of the inner path that leads to the Kingdom of God.

Come walk with me—together we will find joy. My journey continues...

Cultural Pilgrimage

The title of this post may appear to be a misnomer. As we understand it, "culture" means the beliefs, customs, arts, etc. of a particular society, group, place, or time. However, this post is intended only for the purpose of sharing with you some of my journeys and visits to important sites "of historical and cultural significance" on our planet.

Valley of the Kings in Egypt, 8 May 2012.

Human consciousness is individual. It is a personal thing. Therefore, each one of us has individual consciousness of the things around us. Different people are affected differently (if at all) by journeys to places outside and beyond their comfort zones.

Pompeii, Italy (taken on 4 May 2014).

It is not possible for me to share with you all the places I have had the blessing of visiting, but I will try to share some that have (in different ways) materially broadened my horizon and deepened my faith in the process. I am cognizant of the fact and do understand that some readers of my blog may come away having different feelings and conclusions. There are many locations around the world where pivotal events have happened, but I can share only a few and hopefully can update this from time to time. Some of these events occurred as a result of *force majeure*. Others happened as a result of human conflicts.

CAMBODIA

Deriving from the Sanskrit word *nagara* (city), Angkor was the capital of a flourishing empire between the 9th and 15th centuries. The ruins of Angkor are located amid forests and farmland to the north of the Great Lake, Tonle Sap, and near modern-day Siem Reap city in Cambodia. The temples of the Angkor area number over 1,000, but the most magnificent are Angkor Wat and the less known but equally impressive Angkor Thom, which I had the opportunity of visiting in the autumn of 2011.

The foremost Hindu concept is the temple-mountain. Angkor Wat is surrounded by moats and is built in a mountain-like pyramidal shape. It is topped by five towers representing the five peaks of Mount Meru.

Angkor Wat was constructed roughly between 1113 and 1150 by the Khmer king Suryavarman II. It was originally built as a Hindu temple dedicated to the god Vishnu. It gradually moved from Hindu to Theravada Buddhist use, which continues to the present day. An estimated 93 percent of the population of Cambodia follows Theravada Buddhism.

Approaching Angkor Wat.

Going to the upper gallery at Angkor Wat.

As we look from the tower of Angkor Wat.

Devatas (deities) are characteristic of the Angkor Wat style.

A modern-day craftsman at work.

Many statutes of Buddha were added to the already very impressive artwork.

Theravada Buddhist monks.

Angkor Thom is about 7 km north of Siem Reap city and about 2 km from Angkor Wat. The Khmer ruler Jayavarman VII (reigned 1181–1220) devoted much of his energy to religious construction projects. A large number of the awesome temples, including the Bayon (a distinctively Mahayana Buddhist central pyramid), were built during his reign. According to the Wikipedia article on Bayon, "The Bayon's most distinctive feature is the multitude of serene and massive stone faces on the many towers which jut out from the upper terrace and cluster around its central peak."

The article also notes that following the death of Jayavarman VII, "the Bayon was modified and augmented for Hindu and Theravada kings in accordance with their own individual religious preferences."

The South Gate of Angkor Thom.

Bayon, a distinctively Mahayana Buddhist central pyramid.

The temple of Ta Prohm was used as a location in the film *Tomb Raider*.

The Wikipedia article on Ta Prohm notes that "the trees growing out of the ruins are perhaps the most distinctive feature of Ta Prohm and 'have prompted more writers to descriptive excess than any other feature of Angkor'" (in the words of Michael Freeman and Claude Jacques).

The demise of Angkor is a mystery. It has been suggested that several factors contributed to its demise: war with the neighbouring polity, conversion of the society to Theravada/Mahayana Buddhism, overpopulation, and climate change. The difficulty in determining the precise reasons for its collapse lies in the lack of historical documentation. So far, much of its history is derived from the detailed Sanskrit carvings at the polity's temples and from the trade reports with China.

Sanskrit carvings at the polity's temples.

TURKEY

Lycia was a geopolitical region in Anatolia that lay in what is today known as the provinces of Antalya and Muğla in southern Turkey.

Lycian rock tombs.

Lycia has been known to history since the records of Ancient Egypt and the Hittite Empire in the late Bronze Age, but the Ancient Lycians are among the most enigmatic people of antiquity. They left behind very few historical records.

What has so far been discovered reveals the lifestyle of a fascinating people culturally different and distinct from the rest of the ancient world at that time. I had the opportunity to view (albeit from a distance) some of major sites displaying unusual Lycian architecture, including incredible rock-cut tombs carved into the cliff faces that dominate the unspoiled, breath-taking land of Lycia.

For further study, read *Dynastic Lycia: A Political History of Lycians and Their Relations with Foreign Powers, c. 545–362 B.C.*, by Anthony G. Keen.

EGYPT

The Karnak Temple is actually a complex with multiple temples to a variety of Theban gods. The centre of the complex was the Amun (and later Amun-re) Temple. It was the largest temple precinct and possibly the most important in Ancient Egypt. Building at the complex began during the reign of Senusret I in the Middle Kingdom (12th Dynasty, 1971–1926 BC) and continued well into the Ptolemaic (Hellenistic) period.

The Hellenistic kingdom in Egypt was ruled by the Ptolemaic dynasty that Ptolemy I Soter founded after the death of Alexander the Great (in 323 BC) and that ended with the death of Cleopatra VII and the Roman conquest (in 30 BC). The construction of the complex went through almost 1,300 years with at least 30 successive pharaohs adding their individual touches to the complex, such as new temples, shrines, pylons, and detailed carved hieroglyphic inscriptions.

As the Wikipedia article on Karnak notes, "The area around Karnak was the ancient Egyptian *Ipet-isut* ('The Most Selected of Places') and the main place of worship of the eighteenth dynasty Theban Triad with the god Amun as its head."

"And they made their lives bitter with hard bondage, in mortar, and in brick ..." -Exodus 1:14 (KJV) was the lot of the Israelite slaves in Egypt. There is archaeological evidence that the Israelites were living and working in Goshen and Ra'amses (Tell el Dab'a) for 430 years, from 1876–1446 BC.

The Lord told Moses, "Speak unto the children of Israel, that they turn and encamp before Pihahiroth, between Migdol and the sea, over against Baalzephon: before it shall ye encamp by the sea" (Exodus 14:2 (KJV). This would take the Israelites toward the well-defended coastal highway leading to Canaan. This historical event is best known from a relief of Seti I (the father of Ramesses II) in the Karnak Temple. That relief illustrates a series of forts on the route and records each of their names. This was the route that the Israelites tried to avoid after leaving Ra'amses. Exodus 13:17 (KJV) states that the Israelites did not go by the "way of the land of the Philistines": "And it came to pass, when Pharaoh had let the people go, that God led them not *through* the way of the land of the Philistines, although that was near; for God said, Lest peradventure the people repent when they see war, and they return to Egypt."

One famous aspect of Karnak is the Hypostyle Hall in the precinct of Amun-Re, a hall area of 4,650 square metres with 134 massive columns arranged in 16 rows. One hundred twenty-two (122) of these columns are 10 metres tall, and the other twelve are 21 metres tall with a diameter of over 3 meters. Here's a description from the Wikipedia article on the Great Hypostyle Hall:

> The north side of the hall is decorated in raised relief, and was mainly Seti I's work. The southern side of the hall was completed by Ramesses II [Seti'I son] in sunk relief, although he used raised relief at the very beginning of his reign before changing to the sunk relief style and re-editing his own raised reliefs there. Ramesses II also usurped decoration of his father along the main north-south and east-west processional ways of the hall, giving the casual observer the idea that he was responsible for the building. Most of Seti I's reliefs in the northern part of the hall were respected, however.

In AD 323, Constantine accepted Christianity and ordered the closing of pagan temples throughout the Roman Empire. Christian churches were founded among the ruins. The most famous example of this is the reuse of the Festival Hall of Thutmose III, where we were able to see the painted decorations of saints and Coptic inscriptions during our recent visit to Karnak.

Here's an excerpt from "The Bible According to Karnak," published in the Fall 2004 issue of *Bible and Spade* (Associates for Biblical Research). It explains the significance of what we learn from Karnak:

> Much of what we know about Egypt's New Kingdom Pharaohs comes from their statuary and reliefs carved at the Karnak Temple and their mortuary temples and tombs across the river. It is worth emphasizing that the Karnak Temple was not constructed as a public monument designed to teach living object lessons to the citizens of Egypt. Average people were not allowed inside the Temple complex. Consequently, every architectural feature, however massive or beautiful, was designed by each Pharaoh to impress his god; and, possibly, to keep the very powerful priesthood as good allies.

The Mortuary Temple of Amenhotep III is located in the Theban Necropolis on the west bank of the Nile, opposite the city of Luxor. It was built for the pharaoh Amenhotep III. The temple, which was believed to be larger than the complex at Karnak, covered an area of 350,000 square metres. But because it was constructed closer to the river than any of the other mortuary temples, it decayed more quickly.

Today we see very little remains of the complex. Only the Colossi of Memnon—two 18-metre stone statues of Amenhotep that stood at the gateway—are still visible. These massive statutes have stood in the Theban Necropolis for more than 3,500 years. The site has since been included in the World Monument Watch list of endangered sites by the World Monuments Fund.

The twin statutes were made from blocks of quartzite quarried at El-Gabal (near modern-day Cairo) and transported overland for about 675 km to Thebes because they were too heavy to be shipped upstream on the Nile. They have stood in the Theban Necropolis across the River Nile since 1350 BC. On close examination, we saw that the statues are quite damaged, with the facial features virtually unrecognizable.

The eastern-northern figure (the one on my left) has a large crack in the lower half and above the waist.

The original function of the Colossi was to stand guard at the entrance to Amenhotep's Memorial Temple (a massive construct built during the lifetime of the pharaoh), where he was worshiped as a god-on-earth both before and after his departure from this world.

JORDAN

Petra (established as early as 312 BC) was the capital city of the Nabateans. It has been a UNESCO World Heritage site since 1985. UNESCO has described Petra as "one of the most precious cultural properties of man's cultural heritage".

Inhabited since prehistoric times, this Nabataean city situated between the Red Sea and the Dead Sea was an important crossroads between Egypt and Phoenicia. Petra is a half-built (half-carved into the rock) city surrounded by mountains that are riddled with passages and gorges where ancient Eastern traditions blend with Hellenistic architecture.

The Siq, or the main entrance to the ancient city of Petra.

Petra was the Greek name; it referred to the rocky location of the Nabataean capital in the red sandstone mountains of Edom. Edom was a historical region of the Southern Levant located south of Judea and the Dead Sea. Here is some background information from "When People Lived at Petra," by Joseph J. Basile:

> According to 2 Kings and 2 Chronicles, Amaziah led a counter offensive against Edomite raiding parties that had been marauding in his kingdom. He pushed them back into Edom, where they took refuge in a mountain fort called Sela (meaning the Rock; "Petra" is Greek for Rock). Amaziah slew 10,000 men while capturing the fort (2 Kings 14:7); then he threw the survivors of the siege off the mountain to their deaths (2 Chronicles 25:11–12). Early in this century, the massif of Umm el-Biyara, which overlooks the central Petra Valley on the west, was identified as a possible location of biblical Sela. Subsequent excavations on top of the plateau by the British archaeologist Crystal M. Bennett uncovered a small Edomite settlement there, but the earliest datable remains were from the seventh century B.C., a century after Amaziah, thus ruling out Umm el-Biyara as the site of Sela. Nevertheless, Bennett's excavations proved Petra was inhabited in the Iron Age. (*Exploring Jordan*, 2008 Biblical Archaeology Society)

Visitors admiring Al Khazneh, popularly known as "the Treasury".

The name Edom (meaning *red* in Hebrew) was given to Esau, the eldest son of the Hebrew patriarch Isaac. Genesis 25:30 (KJV) states, "And Esau said to Jacob, Feed me, I pray thee, with that same red pottage; for I am faint: therefore was his name called Edom."

The Torah, Tanakh, and New Testament thus describe the Edomites as descendants of Esau. Obadiah prophesied that Edom would be "small among the nations... utterly despised" (Obadiah 1:2). Obadiah's prediction came true in the 5th century BC, when Edom was removed from Petra. The Edomites would later disappear from history completely. God, in his dealings with Edom, kept his promise to his people that "Whoever curses you, I will curse" (Genesis 12:3).

Al Khazneh, hewn into the sandstone cliff

In pre-Islamic times, the Nabataeans worshiped the Arab gods and goddesses as well as a few of their deified kings (for example, Obodas I).

According to Arab tradition, Petra is the spot where Moses struck a rock with his staff and water came forth and where Moses's brother Aaron is buried at Mount Hor, known today as Jabal Haroun or Mount Aaron. The narrow valley at the head of which Petra is sited is called Wadi Musa (Valley of Moses).

In the 4th century AD, nearly 500 years after the establishment of Petra as a trade centre, Christianity found its way there. After the Islamic conquest of 629–632, Christianity in Petra gave way to Islam. Tamás Arany writes in "Haroun Mountain":

> Although Aaron and his final resting place is holy for all the three monotheistic religions of the Jewish, Christians and Islam, till the last decades of the 20th century it was real hard for non-Muslims to pay a visit on the mountain. For its great sanctity for the local people they used to keep a suspicious eye on every foreigner attempting to get there. However nowadays, with a necessary amount of respect and an open mind in a cultural-religious way will help one for sure to gain their trust and they will give their famous natural hospitality and caring help in advance. This trip actually has to be undertaken in a spirit of a pilgrimage and a spiritual journey through history and tradition. (http://nabataea.net/haroun.html)

Petra is usually identified in the Bible as "Sela," which means a *rock* (Judges 1:36 and Isiah 16:1) or "the cleft in the rock" (Obadiah 1:3): "The pride of thine heart hath deceived thee, thou that dwellest in the clefts of the rock, whose habitation is high; that saith in his heart, who shall bring me down to the ground?" In a parallel passage, "Sela" is understood to mean simply "the rock" (2 Chronicles 25:12).

MEXICO

Chichén Itzá, a large pre-Columbian city located in the eastern portion of Yucatán state in Mexico, was built by the Mayan people of the Postclassic period.

The Tzompantli, or Skull Platform.

PILGRIM

Columns in the Temple of a Thousand Warriors.

According to Mayan chronicles, Hunac Ceel (ruler of Mayapan) conquered Chichén Itzá in the 13th century. While some archaeological evidence indicates Chichén Itzá was at one time looted and plundered, there appears to be greater evidence that it could not have been looted by the people of Mayapan (at least not according to some other sources from when Chichén Itzá was an active urban centre).

Archaeological data now indicates that Chichén Itzá had declined as a regional centre by 1250, before the rise of Mayapan. Ongoing research at the site of Mayapan may help resolve this chronological conundrum.

Chichén Itzá was for many years the centre of pilgrimage for the Ancient Mayans. In recent times, the National Institute of Anthropology and History (INAH), which manages the archaeological site of Chichén Itzá, has been closing monuments to public access.

Visitors can walk around the monuments but can no longer climb them or go inside their chambers. The El Castillo had already been closed for over a year when we arrived in the spring of 2008.

CHINA

The Terracotta Warriors and Horses situated east of Xi'an in Shaanxi, China, were discovered on 29 March 1974 by a group of farmers digging a water well. This discovery was one of the most significant discoveries in the 20th century.

Terracotta Warriors and Horses is a collection of terracotta sculptures depicting the armies of Qin Shi Huang, who ruled as the first emperor of the Qin Dynasty from 220 to 210 BC. Qin was also accredited with building the first version of the Great Wall of China. He ruled until his death, which occurred in 210 BC despite his infamous search for an elixir of immortality. The purpose of the terracotta army was to protect the emperor in his afterlife.

At the time of our visit in 2008, four pits had been partially excavated. Three are filled with the terracotta soldiers, horse-drawn chariots, and weapons. The fourth pit is empty, a testament to the original unfinished construction.

Archaeologists estimate the pits contain as many as 8,000 figures, but the total may never be known. According to writings of court historian Sima Qian, the Emperor Qin ordered the construction of the mausoleum shortly after taking the throne. More than 700,000 labourers worked on the project, which was halted in 209 BC amid uprisings a year after Qin's death.

GREECE

The Parthenon was a temple constructed on the Acropolis in Athens, Greece, for the Greek goddess Athena.

Construction of the Parthenon began in 447 BC and took 10 years to complete. It was turned into a Christian church in the 6th century AD. Subsequent to the Ottoman conquest of Athens in 1458, the Parthenon was converted into a mosque.

Ottoman Turks used it for storing gunpowder during the Venetian attack on Athens in 1687. The stores were ignited during the bombardment, causing an explosion that damaged the building. However, its basic structure remains intact, and reconstruction and restorations efforts have been underway.

In 1974, when I first visited the Acropolis, it was not crowded with tourists. In 1975, the Greek government began a concerted effort to restore the Parthenon and other Acropolis structures. Restoring the structural integrity of the edifice is important because the Parthenon is situated in an earthquake-prone region. However, even though damage caused by the explosion will be mitigated, the Parthenon will not be restored to a pre-1687 condition.

I noticed tremendous differences and changes during my recent visit to the Acropolis in the spring of 2014, 40 years after my initial visit. The Parthenon's aesthetic integrity is also being restored by filling in sections of the column drums and lintels (which were chipped) with apparently the same marble sculptured and cemented in place.

CYPRUS

The Land of Aphrodite, the goddess of love, is officially the Republic of Cyprus, an island country in the far eastern Mediterranean Sea and a member of the European Union.

The Rock of Aphrodite (*Petra tou Romiou*) in Paphos.

Seafaring people from the Near East landed their boats on the island of Cyprus some 10,000 years ago. Cyprus, situated at the most eastern end of the Mediterranean, is at the crossroads of three continents: Europe, Asia, and Africa. The location—a meeting point of great civilizations—has been a major factor influencing the course of Cyprus's history.

The earliest known human activity on the island dates to around the 10th millennium BC. Archaeological remains from this period include the well-preserved Neolithic village of Khirokitia, and Cyprus is home to some of the oldest water wells in the world.

Marble statue of Aphrodite in the Cyprus Museum.

Wiccan Horned God in the Cyprus Museum.

Petra tou Romiou, also known as Aphrodite's Rock, is a sea stack in Paphos, Cyprus. The island of Cyprus played a great part in the Greek mythology as the birthplace of Aphrodite.

The statute *Aphrodite of Soli* has become a symbol of Cyprus.

Ayia Napa Monastery.

The Ayia Napa Monastery is now an Ecumenical Conference Centre serving churches in Cyprus and the Middle East.

The culture of Cyprus is divided between the Greek and Turkish Cypriots. Each community maintains its own culture linked to the cultures of Greece and Turkey, and there is little cultural interchange between the two groups.

Distant view of the Greek Orthodox church.

Inside a Greek Orthodox church.

The Greek culture has been present on the island since antiquity. Christians make up 78 percent of the Cypriot population. Most Greek Cypriots and therefore the majority of the population of Cyprus are members of the Autocephalous Greek Orthodox Church of Cyprus.

Inside the Selimiye Mosque.

The Ottoman Empire brought the Turkish culture to the island in 1570. Most of the Turkish Cypriots are officially Sunni Muslim.

The island was conquered by Alexander the Great in 333 BC. Following his death and the subsequent division of his empire among his successors, Cyprus became part of the Hellenistic empire of Ptolemaic Egypt.

Cyprus became a Roman province in 58 BC. Mark Antony gave the island to Cleopatra VII of Egypt, but it became a Roman province again in 30 BC, after his defeat at the Battle of Actium (31 BC). It was in Paphos that Sergius Paulus, the proconsul (Roman governor) of the island province of Cyprus, was converted to Christianity on Paul's first missionary journey (Acts 13:6–13)

Although information about early history is easily available to us, we usually overlook the passages relating to Cyprus. These passages lay down the crucial foundation for us to understand about Barnabas and Paul's mission to spread the Word of Christ among the Gentiles in foreign lands. Acts 13:2 says, "As they ministered to the Lord, and fasted, the Holy Ghost said, separate me Barnabas and Saul for the work where unto I have called them."

St. Paul's Pillar.

After the Ptolemaic dynasty (see the section "Egypt," earlier in this article), the Roman Empire divided into an Eastern half and a Western half, and Cyprus came under the rule of Byzantium. The Arabs invaded Cyprus in force in AD 653 during the Arab–Byzantine wars. In AD 688, the emperor Justinian II and the caliph 'Abd al-Malik reached an unprecedented agreement: for the next 300 years, Cyprus was ruled jointly by both the Arabs and the Byzantines. The Byzantines recovered control over the island for short periods thereafter, but the status quo was always restored.

In 1191 during the Third Crusade, Richard I of England captured the island from Isaac Komnenos of Cyprus. Richard used it as a major supply base that was relatively safe from the Saracens. A year later, Richard sold the island to the Knights Templar, who, following a bloody revolt, in turn sold it to Guy of Lusignan (King of Jerusalem, 1186–1192). As Lord of Cyprus, Guy eventually died in Nicosia in 1194. The descendants of the Lusignans continued to rule the Kingdom of Cyprus until 1474.

UNITED STATES OF AMERICA

Oak Alley Plantation is located in the community of Vacherie, Louisiana. It is one of the most photographed plantations because of its quarter-mile canopied walk lined with a double row of 28 oak trees leading from the Mississippi River. The exterior of the mansion features a freestanding colonnade of 28 Doric columns (on all four sides) that correspond to the oak trees in the alley.

This is a common feature of pre–Civil War (antebellum) mansions of the Mississippi Valley in the South. Construction was of bricks made on-site. The 16-inch walls were finished with stucco on the exterior and were painted white to give the semblance of marble.

The mansion has a square floor plan, organised around a central hall that runs from the front to the rear on both floors.

Oak Alley was initially a sugar cane plantation. Built in 1839, the plantation was originally called *Bon Séjour*, but eventually the iconic tree-lined walk leading to the mansion led to its being renamed Oak Alley.

The rooms feature high ceilings and large windows.

The French introduced African chattel slaves to the territory in 1710 after capturing a number of them as plunder during the War of the Spanish Succession. In order to develop the new territory, the French transported more than 2,000 Africans to New Orleans between 1717 and 1721 on at least eight ships.

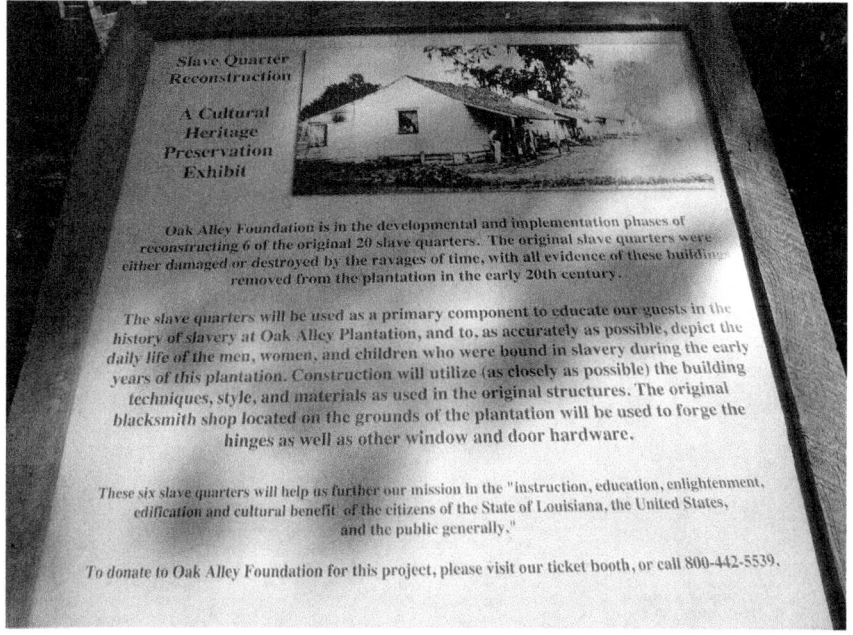

The most noted slave who lived on Oak Alley Plantation was named Antoine. In the inventory of the estate conducted on J. T. Roman's death, he was listed as "Antoine, 38, Creole Negro gardener/expert grafter of pecan trees" with a value of $1,000.

On 18 December 1865, slavery ended in the United States. Secretary of State William Seward issued a statement verifying the ratification of the 13th Amendment to the U.S. Constitution, making the end of slavery official eight months after the end of the Civil War.

RELIGIONS AROUND THE WORLD

According to some estimates, there may be more than 4,000 religions in the world. *Religion* is difficult to define. Perhaps we may simply call it a "cultural system". It is a collection of beliefs and worldviews that relate and connect humanity to spirituality and sometimes (but not always) moral values. Most religions have traditions, narrative symbols, and sacred histories intended to give meaning and purpose to life or to explain the origin of life or the universe. They tend to derive guidelines, ethics, laws, or preferred lifestyles from inspirations or ideas about the cosmos and human nature.

(26 April 2009) The Blue Mosque.

Hurva Synagogue, Jerusalem.

(4 May 2013) A Samoa longhouse. In Samoan mythology, a story about the god Tagaloa, also known as Tagaloa-Lagi (Tagaloa of the Heavens), explains why Samoan houses are round.

(20 May 2012) India.

(14 October 2010) Korea.

(8 March 2011) Hawaii.

(9 March 2011) Hawaii.

(9 March 2011) Hawaii.

(20 May 2010) Japan.

(8 October 2010) China.

(3 May 2013) Samoa.

PILGRIM

PIVOTAL EVENTS IN HUMAN HISTORY (NATURAL OR CAUSED BY HUMAN CONFLICT)

Eruption of Mount Vesuvius

An ancient voice reaches out from the past to tell us about the destruction of Pompeii and the story of the most catastrophic and infamous volcanic eruptions in human recorded history. The only surviving eyewitness account of the event consists of two letters written by Pliny the Younger (who was 17 at the time of the eruption) to the historian Tacitus. According to the online article "The Destruction ofPompeii, 79 AD" on Eye Witness to History, "A few years after the event, Pliny wrote a friend, Cornelius Tacitus, describing the happenings of late August 79 AD when the eruption of Vesuvius obliterated Pompeii."

Pompeii was buried under 4 to 6 metres of ash and pumice after the eruption of Mount Vesuvius. The city was lost for over 1,500 years until its initial discovery in 1599 and a broader rediscovery almost 150 years later by Spanish engineer Rocque Joaquin de Alcubierre in 1748. An estimated 16,000 people died in consequence of the eruption.

Pompeii with Mount Vesuvius towering above.

Excavations have generally ceased due to the moratorium imposed to protect the site. The concern for conservation has continually troubled archaeologists. The objects buried in Pompeii were well-preserved for almost 2,000 years; the lack of air and moisture allowed for the objects to remain underground with little to no deterioration.

Like Pompeii, Herculaneum was buried by the eruption of Mount Vesuvius. However, unlike Pompeii, it was actually more preserved than destroyed by the blast. This means the buildings are in better condition—including many that we saw—giving visitors a more accurate feel for what the city looked like before the eruption. The hot ash that covered Herculaneum sealed frescoes and mosaics on their walls.

War

Harry Emerson Fosdick said that "the tragedy of war is that it uses man's best to do man's worst". There is a need to reconcile this saying with that of Edmond Burke: "All tyranny needs to gain a foothold is for people of good conscience to remain silent." I was born in time of war (WWII) and at some stages in my life have been called a "peacenik". However, war to me really is sometimes necessary—for example, as against Adolf Hitler.

World War I Memorial at Vanuatu, a South Pacific island nation that was then known as New Hebrides.

Pivotal event caused by human conflicts.

Model of the atomic bomb detonated over Nagasaki.

11:02 a.m., 9 August 1945: the moment of the explosion and the instant the city of Nagasaki and its citizens suffered utter devastation.

WWII Memorial at Nagasaki.

Peace be with you,

Nicholas

> "There no more will envy blind us,
>   Nor will pride our peace destroy"
>
> —"As We Gather at Your Table", Carl P. Daw Jr.

Just a thought: Is human conflict the "fruit" of the original sin of man, "pride"?

My journey continues... Come walk with me.

Solitude (Subiaco), Italy

It was the worst of times and the best of times. It was 13 October 2014, and on this day May and I would fly from Vancouver, Canada, to Frankfurt en route to Fiumicino, Italy (Leonardo da Vinci Airport). When I checked in online the night before our departure, I saw we had been assigned seats 13A and 13B.

Some say 13 is an unlucky number and that the 13th is not a good day... we still remember 13 May 1969 in Malaysia-an incident of sectarian violence and riot in Kuala Lumpur Malaysia in which many hundred lives were lost. We also know that at this time many office buildings, hotels, and even cruise ships do not have a 13th floor.

Both of us had learned to travel light—particularly when going on pilgrimage. This was our pilgrimage to Sacro Speco and St. Scholastica's Abbey (a Benedictine territorial abbey in Subiaco,

Italy), founded in the 6th century by St. Benedict of Nursia. The monastery today gives its name to the *Subiaco Congregation*, a grouping of monasteries worldwide that makes up part of the Order of St. Benedict. On this journey, we hoped to have the opportunity to visit the grotto where St. Benedict made his first hermitage... and thereafter to sail from Rome (Civitavecchia) to the Holy Land.

A friend had driven us to Lougheed train station, from which we took the sky train to the Vancouver International Airport (YVR). Our flight was due to depart YVR at 7:00 p.m. for Frankfurt, onwards to Rome. After the plane had taxied out onto the runway (having already been delayed for more than two hours), the captain announced that we had a technical problem and it was necessary for us to return to the airport, where we would have to wait for further announcements. It turned out that an electrical component on the plane needed to be replaced, and it had to be flown in from Toronto. To cut the story short, we were accommodated for the night in the Sheraton Hotel at YVR and finally left YVR the following day (14 October) at 3:00 pm. We still had our assigned seats, 13A and 13B!

Queue at YVR for our flight.

Upon our arrival at Fiumicino Airport via Frankfurt, we discovered (after waiting and searching around all the carousels) that May's luggage had not arrived with us. We reported the missing luggage to the Lufthansa agent and provided them the forwarding address in Civitavecchia (Rome) where we were expected to be on 18 October, after our visit to Subiaco. To amuse May, I said that it was meant to be a test for her—that for the next few days she would have to live the life of a Benedictine nun.

"Everything will be all right" I said.

Naturally, our schedules had all been upset. We were due to arrive Subiaco at 3:00 p.m. but did not make it until 8:00 p.m. By then it was pitch dark. We had not the faintest idea where our lodging was because its address did not show up on the GPS.

As we circled around the country road, we saw a small, dimly lit grocery store by the roadside. I stopped momentarily and tried (with great difficulty) to communicate with the owners. One young couple who was checking out the fruits at the nearby fruit stand overheard our "conversation". They understood that we were looking for directions to Belvedere B&B. They tried to draw us a sketch to show us how to get there, but when they realized it was too complicated, they volunteered to drive their car to lead us through the village of Subiaco, all the way to our lodging. We were very thankful for the kindness of these complete strangers.

When we arrived at Belvedere B&B, the owner told us that she had actually sent her daughter to Subiaco bus station at 3:00 p.m. to meet us. Belvedere B&B turned out to be a gem, sited spectacularly on the side a mountain. It has been run continuously by the same family (on the mother's side) for five generations.

The grandmother (maternal) cooked delectable homemade pasta for us, which we paired with toasty local red wine. We then retired for a restful night after a long and stressful trip from Vancouver, Canada.

    We woke up at the break of dawn to the tranquillity of a countryside environment, not unlike what we had experienced a year ago in this part of the world—the tranquillity of the life we once lived (for a while) along the Camino Francés from the tiny idyllic French village of Saint-Jean-Pied-de-Port to Santiago de Compostela in Galicia, Spain...

Early morning view of the path leading to our lodging.

Belvedere B&B is not recommended for people with mobility problems, but the reward for the climb is a spectacular view!

Our bedroom is third from the right.

There were two monasteries which I had hoped to visit: the Monastero di San Benedetto and the Monastero di Santa Scolastica. The Monastero di San Benedetto (Monastery of St. Benedict) is located a few kilometres above the Scholastica abbey. I decided that we should hike up to Monastero di San Benedetto and then work our way down the mountain. The owner of Belvedere had also informed us that at the foot of the mountain, there was a river (and a waterfall) that flowed into a small lagoon, which she thought we might enjoy visiting as well.

MONASTERY OF ST. BENEDICT

When we arrived at the Monastero di San Benedetto, we were met by Dom Maurizio Viera, OSB (our *coordinatore visite guidate*), who briefed and advised us on how to make our way through this magnificent monastery.

This sanctuary is spectacularly attached to the side of the mountain and supported by nine high arcades. It comprises two churches, one above the other, and several chapels of irregular artistic arrangements with many frescoes and paintings.

Climbing a series of steps to the Monastery of St. Benedict, which is "spluttered" against the rock like a "swallow's nest".

The last few steps.

The first sighting of the monastery as we reached the top of the terrace steps.

Approaching the entrance of the Monastery of St. Benedict.

The monastery seen from the terrace preceding the entrance. The passage leads to the Old Capitular Hall.

The lower church.

Exit of the lower church.

The Rose Garden outside the lower church.

A passage leading to the statute of St. Benedict.

The statue of St. Benedict, who in a gesture of paternal protection, has his arm outstretched towards the rugged rock of Talèo.

The interior is a maze of small chapels and cells (including one over St. Benedict's own hermitage) carved into the living rock and covered by frescoes of various periods; the oldest Byzantine art dates back to the 8th century.

The entrance/Old Capitular Hall.

Stairway to the upper church.

Pilgrims from Germany preparing for Mass.

Another chapel.

One of the many chapels inside.

The main altar is a Cosmati work. The chapel of the main altar takes form from the original cave where it was built. On the right of the altar is the *transetto*, or transept, which shows some interesting frescoes of Benedict's sister Scolastica.

A view to the entrance of the upper church as pilgrims/visitors arrive.

One of the most interesting points is the representation of St. Francis of Assisi—the oldest known portrait of the saint in existence. It was actually drawn before his death, and it dates back to St. Francis's retreat to Subiaco (1223–1224). He is depicted without the stigmata and without a halo. The fresco has a magnificent simplicity that reveals with remarkable vividness the humble and serene spirit of the great Saint of Assisi.

The fresco of St. Francis of Assisi encased.

In the lower church is the entrance to the Holy Cave (Sacro Speco). We then entered this grotto where St. Benedict (we learned) retired to hermetic life for three years with only the help of the monk Romanus, who lowered down to him food by a long rope from the edge of the overtopping rock. This is the main point of reference of the shrine.

The Grotto of St. Benedict. Thomas Merton writes, "There is nothing whatsoever of the ghetto spirit in St. Benedict. That is the wonderful thing about the Rule and about Benedict himself, the freshness, the freedom, the sanity, the broadness, and the healthiness of the Benedictine life."

The *Rule of St. Benedict* answers the question of how we ought to live our lives.

This holistic approach calls for:

- A balance of prayer, work, and leisure
- Stability and commitment lived in community in which Christ is seen in each person
- Stewardship of all created things which come from the hand of God
- Hospitality which receives and cares for each person as Christ

Much has already been written about the Gospel values of the *Rule of St. Benedict*. These values stand in contrast to the values of our society (which are listed in brackets):

> Seeking God (seeking material things) + The common good (individualism) + Commitment (non-involvement) + Mutual sharing (competition) + Hospitality (rejection) + Care (exploitation) + Peace (violence)

ST. SCHOLASTICA'S ABBEY

We left the Monastero San Benedetto and descended to the bottom of the mountain to look for the river and the lagoon that the owner of Belvedere had mentioned to us. We spent some time at this serene spot and then made our way...

...up to St. Scholastica's Abbey (also known as Subiaco Abbey). St. Scholastica's Abbey was named after St. Benedict's sister, herself a monastic. Scholastica was also born in Nursia, Umbria, in 480. She and her brother Benedict were brought up together until he left to pursue studies in Rome.

Benedict lived in Subiaco for about 30 years. He spent three years as a hermit in a cave (*Sacro Speco*) and the rest in a community. During this time, he founded here 13 monasteries. Today, only one monastery remains: Saint Scholastica's Abbey.

This monastery of St. Scholastica (*Proto-Cenobio Benedettino*) is the most ancient Benedictine monastery in the world. It is arranged around three cloisters. The oldest, from the 12th and 13th centuries, is in the Cosmatesque style and is the most harmonious. The second, which is in the Gothic style, dates to the 14th and 15th centuries. The third is from the late 16th century, and it is in Renaissance style. The abbey church is Gothic with a Roman-style campanile (entirely rebuilt in 1771–1776 in a Neoclassical style) that stands apart from the rest of the abbey's architecture.

The monastery entrance.

The second cloister is in Gothic style and dates back to the beginning of the 14 century. It was built in an irregular shape with a kind of travertine (limestone) called *cardellino*.

The first cloister is in Renaissance style. It was built between the 16th and the 17th centuries (1580–1689).

The Romanesque cloister is the oldest one, and it dates back to the 12th century. It is a Cosmatan cloister because of the family who built it (a very well-known family at that time). We remain thankful for their beautiful works with marble and especially with mosaics.

The Benedictine Sisters of St. Scholastica Monastery follow the *Rule of St. Benedict*, as do Benedictines throughout the world. Written by St. Benedict in the 6th century, the *Rule* is a practical and spiritual guide to living a life for God and others according to the teaching of the Gospels.

The beautiful Romanesque Bell Tower is one of the oldest towers in this part of Italy. Its base was built in the 9th century, and the tower was finished in the 11th century.

In the 9th century, St. Scholastica's Abbey was twice destroyed by the Saracens (in 828–829 and 876–877). It was later restored, and it grew in the 10th century thanks to the patronage of several popes, many of whom were in fact Benedictine monks. There is a magnificent library, which we wished we had had the time to visit.

Today, St. Scholastica's Abbey holds a place in the *Subiaco Congregation*, a grouping of 64 male Benedictine monasteries on five continents (to which 54 female monasteries also belong) within the larger Benedictine Confederation.

Scholastic is the term commonly used to describe the philosophy of the Christian Middle Ages, in which it developed; that school of thought is also known as *scholasticism*.

A view of St. Scholastica's Abbey as we departed Subiaco.

Esther de Waal writes, "This man [St. Benedict] gives us a sign, a promise and a challenge as much today as when the Rule was written. Shall we in our generation be able to handle the gift of Benedict's Rule with respect, reverence and responsibility and share this gift with others?"

The beautiful village of Subiaco. We caught sight of this beautiful village in the early morn the following day.

We say "addio", but it will always remain in my mind and heart as a place of inspiration and harmony, a spiritual source, a place to suspend our false egos...

We left Subiaco and made our way to the port of Civitavecchia.

Everything did turn out to be all right for us. May went back to live her nonmonastic life. Her "lost suitcase" was waiting for her at Civitavecchia as we arrived from Subiaco to set sail for the Holy Land.

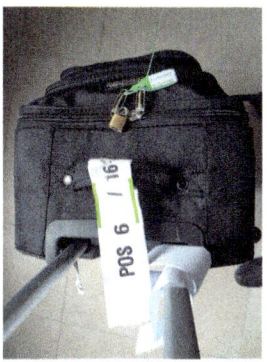

We set sail for the Holy Land.

Peace be with you,

Nicholas

My journey continues...

The Holy City: Understanding the Past

It was 24 October 2014. A day on which I would be visiting the most important sites in Jerusalem to feel the "presence" of the Holy City and perhaps seek to understand why Jerusalem is "everything" to the three monotheistic religions of Judaism, Islam, and Christianity.

The Old City of Jerusalem is divided into four sections (clockwise as follows): The Jewish Quarter, the Armenian Quarter, the Christian Quarter, and the Muslim Quarter. Despite the fluid situation in the Middle East (in Israel in particular), somehow tens of thousands of people make their way there every year, and pilgrimage to the Holy Land continues.

Joining tour groups is not normally my cup of tea because I find them too regimented and restrictive. Following and listening to a tour guide does not give me the opportunity for personal reflection or sufficient time to take photographs of interest to me. However, because of security reasons in Israel, I had decided that we would join a day tour for the journey into Jerusalem. On this particular day, our organised tour was to take us to the Old City of Jerusalem after visiting the Garden of Gethsemane. However, because of extenuating circumstances (which I will explain later in this article), we did not have the opportunity to enter Gethsemane.

Our journey into the Holy Land began from Ashdod, the port city of Israel to which we had earlier sailed from Rome (Civitavecchia). Since we were to travel to and approach Jerusalem from Ashdod by coach, our journey would first take us to the Mount of Olives towards Gethsemane. The Mount of Olives is actually two hilltops perched east of the Temple Mount and west of the Judean desert. It was midmorning when we first caught sight of the Holy City from afar, with the Dome of the Rock conspicuously dazzling under the morning sun.

A distant view of the Holy City.

By the time we reached the Mount of Olives, the road leading to Gethsemane had already been cordoned off because it was Friday—an important day for Muslims to attend prayers at the nearby Al-Aqsa Mosque. Since we were not permitted to enter Gethsemane at that time, it became necessary for us to reschedule. Our guide therefore made adjustments to our itinerary, and we left the Mount of Olives with the intention of coming back to Gethsemane later in the afternoon. Our driver then took us to the Jaffa Gate outside the Old City of Jerusalem.

From Gethsemane to Jaffa Gate.

Approaching Jaffa Gate.

We disembarked outside the wall and continued our journey on foot into the Old City through the Jaffa Gate to David Street. We then turned left into the Christian Quarter.

Greek Catholic Patriarchate Street.

Christian Quarter Street.

Mosque of Omar.

We walked along the Greek Catholic Patriarchate Street and continued walking until we saw the Mosque of Omar. And then we walked through the arch into the plaza of the Holy Sepulchre. We learned that in AD 33, when Jesus was tried and crucified by Pontius Pilate (Roman procurator of Judea from AD 26–36), this spot lay outside the Old City wall (not to be confused with the current 16th-century wall). It was just outside the Garden Gate—the garden cemetery mentioned in the Gospel of John: "Now in the place where he was crucified there was a garden; and in the garden a new sepulchre, wherein was never man yet laid" (John 19:41). Liturgical celebrations were held here until the First Jewish Revolt against Rome beginning in AD 66, when many Jerusalem Christians fled for safely to the city of Pella (in modern Jordan).

The plaza of the Holy Sepulchre.

The arch of the Holy Sepulchre.

The early Jerusalem Christian community never lost its memory of the place where Christ was crucified and buried. Constantine began building the first church on the spot in 326. The church was set on fire by the Persians in 614 and was reconstructed by Modestus, a Greek Orthodox Patriarch of Jerusalem. When the Muslims took control of Jerusalem in 638, the church came under the protection of two ruling dynasties, the Umayyad and the Abbasid, until it was once again destroyed by Fāṭimid caliph al-Ḥākim in 1009. The current church was constructed in 1012–1170.

The entrance to the Church of Holy Sepulchre.

The Stone of Unction (Anointing).

This modern Greek Orthodox mosaic hangs behind the Stone of Unction (Anointing) and can be seen as we enter the church.

We entered the Church of the Holy Sepulchre, which is believed to enshrine the sites of Christ's crucifixion, entombment, and resurrection. As soon as we passed through the entrance door, the Stone of Unction appeared before us. The stone is not ancient but was placed here in 1810, after a fire destroyed the previous stone that had been here since the time of the Crusaders in the 1100s. It is a traditional commemoration of the preparation of Jesus's body for burial (the focus of modern Orthodox Christian veneration), which I, born and raised in the Lutheran tradition, had come to appreciate.

Ascending Golgotha.

We took a sharp turn to ascend what is left of Golgotha after 2,000 years of wear by pilgrims and tear by visitors and others—the steps are worn with shallow dips, and the stairs tilt slightly to the left. These are the 18 steps up to Calvary. The rock of Calvary is located a few feet on the other side of this wall, but once we reached the top of the steps, we entered and saw underneath the high Greek Orthodox altar the mount upon which Christ was crucified. A hole under the altar allows one to touch in veneration the bedrock of Calvary at a spot that is traditionally believed to be near the place where the base of the cross was placed. On both sides of the altar we could see (through the viewing glass) the original bedrock of Calvary: Golgotha, or "The Skull".

The high Greek Orthodox altar. Underneath the altar is the bedrock of Calvary at a spot that is traditionally believed to be near the place where the base of the cross was placed.

The faithful queuing to touch the bedrock.

The faithful touching the bedrock of Calvary in veneration.

We learned from the historian Josephus's description of the Garden Gate and the early Byzantine tradition that Jesus was flogged near the Zion Gate of the Armenian Quarter (see "Armenian Quarter" later in this post). Below the Church of Holy Sepulchre was a hilly, abandoned limestone rock quarry. Archaeological evidence revealed that in ancient times, abandoned limestone quarries often were turned into cemeteries. Joseph of Arimathea had dug a tomb that he gave to Christ—see Matthew 27:59-61 (also Mark 15:46-47 and Luke 23:53).

The dome of the Rotunda. This is the inside the larger grey dome of the Church of the Holy Sepulchre.

The Rotunda.

Right in the middle of the Rotunda in the Holy Sepulchre is the Tomb of Jesus.

The Aedicula. The current shrine over the tomb (replacing a series of shrines going back to the 4th century) dates only to 1810.

For this reason in the Church of the Holy Sepulchre, the tomb (managed by the Greek Orthodox Church, which dates back to the book of Acts) is close to Golgotha, and there is a Greek Orthodox chapel with a knee-high pillar and a circular button marking it as halfway between Calvary and the tomb.

Today when we entered this enormous church to ascend Golgotha, we were also able to descend to and walk around the Rotunda to visit the tomb under the roof of one enormous church (as it is currently defined). In 1009, the caliph al-Ḥākim destroyed the Church of the Holy Sepulchre and crushed the stone block around the tomb that had been left by Constantine, though eyewitnesses reported that the tomb chamber was left intact.

We learned that the key to the Church of Holy Sepulchre (the holiest spot in Christendom) was given to two Muslim families 800 years ago; it remains in their keeping, and they still open the church every morning at dawn and lock it at dark. On the Via Dolorosa, we met one of the men from these families.

The man who holds the key to the Church of Holy Sepulchre.

Part of the Via Dolorosa that we walked on today was created by the Crusaders, who brought the 14 Stations of the Cross from Roman Catholic Europe (see the section "Armenian Quarter" later in this post). The Crusaders assumed that the *lithostrotos* (pavement) beneath the monastery of the French Sisters of Zion was the pavement of the Antonia Fortress, which they mistook for the praetorium where Jesus was tried before Pontius Pilate. However, archaeologists dated that pavement to Hadrian's reconstruction of the city in AD 135.

Alternative routes are followed by those with different opinions about the path Jesus took. For some pilgrims, the actual route taken by Jesus along the Via Dolorosa is of smaller importance. The pilgrimage itself—with the reflection on the events along the way due to the proximity to the sites—has greater and deeper meaning attached.

DOME OF THE ROCK

The Dome of the Rock was built between 688 and 691 by Umayyad caliph 'Abd al-Malik. It is the first major sanctuary built by Islam and the only one to have survived essentially intact. It is believed that 'Abd al-Malik wanted to usurp Judaism and Christianity by claiming the Temple spot.

The Crusaders converted it into a church that they called the Temple of The Lord, but Saladin removed the altar and converted it back into a mosque in 1187. The second staircase to the left is now off-limits to non-Muslims. On this occasion, we did not have the opportunity to enter the Dome but were able to look to the far northwest corner to the tall minaret that is part of a Muslim school.

JEWISH QUARTER

The Temple Mount (Har Ha-Bayit or Haram esh-Sharif) and the Western Wall (Hakotel HaMa'aravi).

The Temple Mount is holy to Jews, Christians, and Muslims. Solomon built the Temple here (2 Chronicles 3:1), on the site where Abraham went to sacrifice Isaac (Genesis 22). The first Temple was destroyed by the Babylonians in 586 BC and then rebuilt in 516 BC (under the auspices of prophets Haggai and Zechariah).

The current Temple esplanade (the open stretch area) is Herodian. Herod expanded the Temple Mount with immense and strong retaining walls, part of which survive today.

Christ broke down the barrier between Jews and Gentiles, as noted in Ephesians 2:14 ("For he himself is our peace who has made both one and has broken down the middle wall of separation.") and Ephesians 2:17–18 ("For he came and preached peace to you who were afar off and to those who were near. For through Him we both have access by one Spirit to the Father.").

Today we were able to enter and visit the Jewish Quarter. After passing through tight security checks, we were able to visit the Wailing Wall, or Kotel—albeit that is only one-eighth (180 feet) of the Western Wall.

Approaching security checkpoints.

Going through security checkpoints.

The huge bevelled stones which extend well beneath ground level are Herodian. The medium-sized stones are from the 7th century, while the small ones at the top were restoration after the earthquake of AD 1033. This western bottom of Herod's retaining wall that surrounded the Temple survived as the holiest place in Judaism.

There is a separate section of the wall for women. It is traditional to write a prayer on a small piece of paper and place it in the cracks of the wall.

The Western Wall (180 feet or 55 metres).

The men's quarter with some visitors perhaps trying to visualize the event that led to the second destruction of the Temple by the Romans in AD 70, which resulted major in historical upheavals that would eventually affect the Abrahamic religions.

The women's quarter.

On this Friday, I was able to take photographs but was given to understand that no writing or photography is allowed in the Western Wall Plaza in the men's quarter on Shabbat (the Sabbath) due to Jewish law.

For more information on the Western Wall, visit http://english.thekotel.org.

Hurva Synagogue.

Many important archaeological finds have been made along the Cardo Maximus and its network of alleyways.

ARMENIAN QUARTER

After leaving the Jewish Quarter, we passed the open excavation of Cardos Maximus into the Armenian Quarter. The excavated Cardo Maximus (a 150-metre stretch) can be seen in an open air section in the heart of the Jewish Quarter between HaYehudim Street and Habad Street. This section is 2.5 metres under the modern street level. Its width is 22.5 metres, and it is flanked by a row of 5-metre-high pillars on both sides of the road.

I was wondering why there was an Armenian Quarter in Old Jerusalem until I learned that Armenia (situated below Russia and next to Turkey) had already been converted to Christianity before the end of 3rd century and was the first nation to do so. From Zion Gate, we make our way along the Armenian Orthodox Patriarchate Road, passing David's Tower Museum (The Citadel) and going back to Jaffa Gate.

In this area stood Herod's palace, which became the praetorium (Matthew 27:27 and Mark 15:16) of the Roman procurator after Herod's son fell out of favour with Rome in AD 6. This was where Jesus was tried by Pontius Pilate and was marched out ("the Way of the Cross") to Golgotha (currently the Church of Holy Sepulchre). It is also where the garden cemetery mentioned in the Gospel of John lies (John 19:41). While the Holy Sepulchre is currently inside the 16th-century walls, it was outside the city walls at the time of Jesus's trial circa AD 33.

The view of this section from the Cardo Street level. The modern street and the Jewish quarter houses are seen above the Cardo.

GARDEN OF GETHSEMANE

After our visit to the Old City, we attempted for the second time to enter the Garden of Gethsemane, but we were once again prevented from doing so. As we were approaching the area, several masked individuals, some with hoods, ran towards our coach. They were preventing us from entering the area for reasons beyond my comprehension.

Aggressors still running towards us as we retreated.

These were aggressive and violent individuals. They were hurling rocks at our coach. Whoever these masked individuals were, they would have recognised (known) that our coach was just a tour bus carrying a group of harmless and peaceful pilgrims/tourists /visitors.

I was sitting in the third row. I heard the thudding sound of the rocks against the windshield before I saw the attackers. We realized that we were being attacked without provocation. The rocks were hurled at our coach, flying in succession. I understand that in Israel due to terrorist attacks on buses, general bus builders have some commercial buses retrofitted with bulletproof glass. I wasn't sure whether our coach was specially fitted, but the windshield remained intact, with only visible scratch marks left behind by the projectiles.

We were stunned and in shock. It took me a few seconds to recollect myself before I managed to make use of my camera. The atmosphere was very tense. Our driver kept his cool and reversed the coach out of the danger zone. The security personnel, who were actually around while we were retreating, restrained themselves and refrained from taking actions against the offenders.

Events such as the one we witnessed are seldom reported by the biased media. We were informed that three days prior to our arrival in Jerusalem, a young driver identified as a 21-year-old from the East Jerusalem neighbourhood of Silwan was shot by security forces after he rammed his car into a train station, injuring seven and killing a baby in the process. It was the second such deadly attack with a vehicle in the city in just under three months.

The tense situation flared into a full-fledged riot a week after our visit, and by the time we arrived in Corinth from the Holy Land, we learned that the government had found it necessary to close the Holy City for the first time in 14 years. It was subsequently reopened for men over 50 and women, with legislation being put in place to impose stiff sentences for those found guilty of stone-throwing.

Somehow despite this unpleasant incident that I experienced at Gethsemane, there was a contrasting picture in my mind. I recalled that during my journey to Antakya (Antioch) Turkey in 2009 (see the earlier post "Steps of Paul"), two very friendly Muslims, who were random acquaintances, took me on their motorbike to St. Peter's Cave Church, the façade of which had been built by the Crusaders during their occupation after the siege of Antioch in the First Crusade.

"Jerusalem, Jerusalem, you who kill the prophets and stone those sent to you, how often I have longed to gather your children together, as a hen gathers her chicks under her wings, and you were not willing."

—Matthew 23:37 (NIV)

Will there be willingness?

Peace be with you,

Nicholas

Just a thought: The Spirit guides us if we are willing. Blessings come in many forms. People come into our lives unexpectedly and for a reason. On this pilgrimage to the Holy Land, we were blessed with the opportunity to cross paths with Ed and Sarah from Nashville, Tennessee, whom we met for the first time. Ed and Sarah introduced us to Lamontte M. Luker, a professor of Hebrew Scriptures at Lutheran Theological Southern Seminary in Columbia, South Carolina. Dr. Luker also serves as faculty associate in the Department of Religious Studies at the University of South Carolina and as adjunct professor of Old Testament at the Jerusalem Center for Biblical Studies. We were invited as guests to his lectures, and he shared his immense knowledge with us as students in the Bible Lands.

My thoughts are also on cyber-archaeology. *Cyber-Archaeology in the Holy Land,* by Thomas E. Levy et al., concludes with these words:

> We should not lose sight of what drives our quest to perfect Cyber-Archaeology in the field and lab: historical and cultural questions that lie at the center of anthropology, history and other fields. The new developments in digital technologies and their relative low costs have made it essential for archaeologists to figure out ways to ingest, manage, curate, analyze, publish and share these large datasets with colleagues and the public. We believe the Cyber-Archaeology research in Jordan will not only reshape research in the southern Levant, but also the broader world of archaeology.

My journey continues...

The Road to Ancient Corinth

On 28 October 2014, we arrived at Athens (the port of Piraeus) by ship from the Holy Land on our way back to Fort Lauderdale, Florida. Because our ship was to be docked for only 12 hours (time constraints), we decided to join a day tour into the ancient city of Corinth. Corinth is about 78 kilometres (48 miles) west of Athens. It is situated on a peninsula, a stretch of land that joins the Peloponnese to the southernmost part of mainland Greece. Our tour to the ancient city included a side trip to visit the Corinth Canal.

The Acrocorinth overlooking the modern Greek Orthodox Church.

THE CORINTH CANAL

The coach took us along the coastal road of the Saronic Gulf to the Corinth Canal. The Corinth Canal, completed in 1893 cuts through the Isthmus of Corinth, effectively making the former peninsula an island. Similar to the Panama Canal, even though on a much smaller scale, the Corinth Canal between the Gulf of Corinth and the Saronic Gulf provides an alternative and much shorter nautical route to the west from Athens (the port of Piraeus) and saves seagoing vessels an immense amount of time.

In antiquity, several rulers had dreamed of digging a cutting through the isthmus. But because of financial and technical difficulties, the Corinth Canal was not completed until towards the end of the 19th century. The side trip to see this Canal therefore was an eye-opener. Immediately after we arrived at the Isthmia pier, we boarded a boat (Catamaran) that had been waiting for us to take us for a round-trip cruise along the canal.

The Isthmia pier.

The Corinth Canal, a dream envisioned a couple thousand years ago, was finally built and completed in 1893. It spans a distance of 6.3 kilometres, and the depth of the canal is 8 metres. The canal width alters between a minimum of 21 metres and a maximum of 25 metres at the bottom and at the surface, respectively. It is surrounded by tremendous high vertical walls. Traversing the canal saves a ship a journey of 185 nautical miles.

Looking back to the Isthmia pier.

The isthmus walking bridge above the canal.

On the way back to Isthmia Pier

Refreshments on the Catamaran

ANCIENT CORINTH

Ever since my journey into Turkey in 2009 ("Steps of Paul"), I have always wanted to visit the ancient city of Corinth. From the New Testament perspective on human conflicts and divisions (even among Christians), Corinth is a focal point and always comes to my mind.

St. Paul visited Corinth in the 50s AD and wrote two letters to the Corinthians (1 and 2 Corinthians in the New Testament). According to Acts of the Apostles, St. Paul lived in Corinth for 18 months, and it was here that he became acquainted with Aquila and Priscilla, who became his fellow workers.

The acropolis of Corinth is known as Acrocorinth. It rises about 1,800 feet above the surrounding plain. At the highest summit was the Temple of Aphrodite.

Ancient Corinth flourished as a major Greek city after first being inhabited in the Neolithic Period (5000–3000 BC). In 146 BC, the Romans destroyed this prosperous Greek city in the Battle of Corinth, a battle fought between the Republic of Rome and Corinth (with its allies in the Achaean League). In 44 BC, under Julius Caesar, the city was rebuilt as a Roman city.

Today, the ruins of ancient Corinth can be seen spread around the base of Acrocorinth, where lay the temple of the Greek goddess Aphrodite, of which little remains. Most of the surviving construction we see is actually Roman (rebuilt by Caesar) rather than Greek. Over the centuries, earthquakes have also destroyed much of the city.

Temple of Apollo (Greek) overlooking the Roman Agora.

The most noticeable remaining ruin of Greek buildings that we saw was the stone Temple of Apollo, constructed on a hill that overlooks the remains of the Roman Agora (marketplace). The temple was still functioning at the time of St. Paul (in the 50s AD) until it was destroyed by earthquakes. Seven of the original Doric columns still stand.

Temple of Octavia (Roman).

A few pillars of the Temple of Octavia (remains of the Roman construction) can also be seen standing today. The temple known by scholars as Temple E was dedicated to the sister of Emperor Augustus (27 BC–AD 14). Roman emperors were treated as gods, and the imperial cult of Rome spread through Europe during the time of St. Paul.

As the Roman Empire developed, along with it came the gradual and formal development of the imperial cult that constituted the worship of the Roman emperor as a god. This practice began at the start of the empire under Augustus, and it became a significant element of Roman religion at that time.

A few years ago when I observed conflicts happening within our contemporary Church, I used to think that we would be on the right track if we went back to the "early Church". In 2009, I journeyed all the way to Tarsus (the birthplace of Paul) and then to Antioch in modern-day Antakya (to the root of Christianity). It was in Antioch that the followers of Christ were first called *Christians*, and the city was the headquarters of the missionary works of Paul in 50s AD. However, as I delved deeper into the past of ancient Corinth on my journey, it had me thinking and realizing that similar problems had actually also plagued the early Church.

As we read through Paul's letters to the Corinthians, we can perceive some of the following divisive issues: pride (a human emotion many of us continue to struggle with), jealousy, sexual immorality, selfishness, participation in cultic meals, and the worship of idols and false gods... the Corinthian Christians were clearly conforming to the norms of worldly behaviour and cultic patterns of the larger society at that time. In his first letter (written during his time in Ephesus), Paul wrote: "Now this I say, that every one of you saith, I am of Paul; and I of Apollos; and I of Cephas; and I of Christ" (1 Corinthians 1:12, KJV) and "For ye are yet carnal: for whereas there is among you envying, and strife, and divisions, are ye not carnal, and walk as men?" (1 Corinthians 3:3, KJV). Paul's letter to the Corinthians reflects the difficulty—even in the early Church—of maintaining a Christian Church in a cosmopolitan and prosperous city like Corinth.

The Acrocorinth can be seen from the Lechaion Road.

Somewhere it is mentioned that archaeology is about excitement and "intellectual curiosity and finding ways to turn that curiosity into knowledge about people in the past". I tried to imagine and visualize the hedonistic lifestyle in this prosperous city of Corinth in the time of Paul. I saw and walked upon the paved Lechaion Road a few metres from the gateway to the south of the Roman Agora. On both sides were small pavements fitted with gutters, which apparently were the artificial recipients of rainwater. The road, including the sidewalks and drainage channels, was actually quite wide: about 12 metres. The steps along the road indicated to me that this passage was probably not intended for vehicles with wheels, even though chariots were in use at that time. Walking up and down this broad marble avenue, I could view the Acrocorinth (and conjured up a picture of the Greek Temple of Aphrodite and heard the noise in the Roman Agora) and could even smell the ocean breeze from the Gulf of Corinth.

Did I take anything away from this journey of mine into the ancient city of Corinth?

In the conclusion of my blog post "Cultural Pilgrimage", I struggled with the following question: Is human conflict the "fruit" of the original sin of man, "pride"? On my way home on this voyage, I had the opportunity to listen to James W. Kennedy, the former director of the JFK Space Center, talk about the "good ego" (inspired by stories of space exploration). Many years ago, as a young man, I read William Shakespeare's *Henry V*, in which he penned this famous line: "Self-love, my liege, is not so vile a sin, as self-neglecting." I have been trying ever since to understand what Shakespeare really meant. It is said that "pride is a conundrum": simultaneously evil and a blessing. We take pride in and also encourage our children to take pleasure in their hard-won successes; still, we consider pride the worst of the seven deadly sins. We need the spiritual gift of discernment to understand the difference between "evil pride" and the "good ego". Human conflicts, without transformation of the beings, will continue to exist everywhere in the world.

I was blessed with the opportunity to walk with humility on the Lechaion Road in ancient Corinth. I fulfilled the wish that I had had when I was in Tarsus. I did it! Someone once said, "I hear, I forget. I see, I remember. I do, I understand." Do I really understand? Did I take anything away from this Journey of mine into the ancient city of Corinth?

Peace be with you,

Nicholas

Just a thought: In 1 Corinthians 3:16-21 (KJV), I still can hear St. Paul's meaningful, strong, and striking words:

> Know ye not that ye are the temple of God, and that the Spirit of God dwelleth in you? If any man defile the temple of God, him shall God destroy; for the temple of God is holy, which temple ye are. Let no man deceive himself. If any man among you seemeth to be wise in this world, let him become a fool, that he may be wise. For the wisdom of this world is foolishness with God. For it is written, He taketh the wise in their own craftiness. And again, The Lord knoweth the thoughts of the wise, that they are vain. Therefore let no man glory in men.

> I hear Paul, but do I listen?

Journey to the New World (*Mundus Novus*)

"I cannot remember the books I've read any more than the meals I have eaten; even so, they have made me."

—Ralph Waldo Emerson

Sometimes we read what we like. Oftentimes, we become what we read or watch on TV or whatever streamed onto our computers. I seldom watch TV, but sometimes I cheat! I don't really read. I just turn pages of the book to find out about the ending first. So you may do the same by scrolling down this blog post to read the ending first. It may or may not surprise you.

On 1 November 2014, I embarked on my journey from the Eternal City to the New World. While Amerigo Vespucci—an explorer, cartographer, navigator, and financier from Florence, Italy (1454–1512)—has been credited with coming up with the term *Mundus Novus* (giving it the popular cachet) in a 1503 letter, similar terms had nevertheless been used and applied many years before him. The Vespucci term *Mundus Novus* label merely applied to the continental landmass of South America. But today when one speaks of the New World in the historical context, Christopher Columbus comes to mind. Columbus completed four round-trip voyages between Spain and the Americas, marking the beginning of the European exploration of the American continent.

There have been many changes since the time of Columbus. In his letter to King Ferdinand, Columbus, describing the result of his first voyage, wrote, "I write this to you, from which you will learn how in thirty-three days I passed from the Canary Islands to the Indies, with the fleet which the most illustrious King and Queen, our Sovereigns, gave to me." As I embarked for the New World, I would be sailing on an immensely more comfortable and faster seagoing vessel. My voyage would take me from Rome, Italy (Civitavecchia), to the eastern shore of the North American continent (Fort Lauderdale) in less than two weeks.

But something has not changed for more than four hundred years. Like Columbus who passed through the Canaries and anchored at the Port of Las Palmas, we too have to pass the Canaries, docking at Port Santa Cruz de Tenerife before crossing the Atlantic. The Canaries are a Spanish Archipelago (one of the 17 autonomous communities) situated just off the southwest coast of mainland Morocco. According to our designated nautical route as shown on the map, before reaching the Canaries, we would be calling at Livorno/Pisa in the picturesque province of Tuscany, Italy, and then sail onwards to Toulon in quaint Provence, France; to the historical Barcelona, Spain; and penultimately to the charming island of Palma de Mallorca, Spain, in this order.

I felt tremendously happy to be able to put my foot forward to walk on new grounds, adapt myself to new surroundings and situations, and see things for the first time (only the beauty in them, because I saw them for the first time). I journeyed to all these distant lands (visiting new and strange places) and received in return (with thanks and gratitude) the many blessings which life so generously presented me as I continued to seek them.

The entrance to Piazza dei Miracoli (Square of Miracles).

Pisa is a city in Tuscany, Central Italy, known worldwide for its leaning tower. Within the metropolitan area, there are also more than 20 historic churches and several palaces.

The Leaning Tower of Pisa, originally conceived to be a bell tower of the cathedral.

It is true that there are things that we cannot Google, and Google cannot show us everything that we are in search of and for. I was blessed with the opportunity to walk upon the ground of another UNESCO Heritage Site, the remarkable Piazza dei Miracoli (Square of Miracles). Like many before me, I saw with my very eyes and was mesmerized by the renowned Torre Pendente (Leaning Tower), a structure that was originally conceived as the cathedral's bell tower and that I had dreamed of seeing at a very young age.

I also had learned that construction of the tower occurred in three stages across a long period of 199 years. The work on the ground floor of the white marble campanile actually started in 1173, and the tower then started leaning due to an inadequate foundation and the subsidence of the soft ground on one side of its base. A project to keep the tower from leaning more and tipping over had only finally been successfully concluded in 2001.

The Old Port of Marseille has been a seaport for 2,000 years.

Marseille is the second largest city in France after Paris.

Marseille has been a fishing port for more than 2,000 years. We visited the Notre-Dame de la Garde, a Catholic basilica which was constructed in 1853–1864 to replace an earlier church of the same name built in 1214. This Neo-Byzantine church (consecrated on 5 June 1864) was constructed on the foundations of an ancient fort located at the highest natural point in Marseille. Sitting majestically on a 149-metre limestone outcrop, it is a major landmark and the site of a popular pilgrimage (held annually on 15 August).

Ascending the steps to the Notre-Dame de la Garde.

A view from the Notre-Dame de la Garde.

Cassis is a commune situated east of Marseille in the Provence–Alpes–Côte-d'Azur region in southern France. It is famous for its high cliffs and the sheltered inlets. It is a popular destination for tourists, some of whom would come to enjoy the wine of Cassis, which are white and rosé.

Cap Canaille, a headland situated in southern France between the towns Cassis and La Ciotat, is the highest bluff in Europe and has been a sailor's landmark for thousands of years.

Cassis is situated on the Mediterranean coast about 20 kilometres (12.4 miles) east of Marseille.

The pleasant inlet of Cassis.

The Stone of Cassis, which was quarried here since antiquity, made the town famous. Industry has since given way to tourism and wine making. Cassis was one of the first three vineyards to profit from the appellation d'origine contrôlée (AOC) introduced in 1936.

We had to try the crêpes someone praised.

The crêpes reminded me of the Crêpes Suzette we once had (long ago) at Jesselton Hotel.

Sanary-sur-Mer, unlike most small towns on the coast of the Mediterranean, is an active village all year round. As a tourist rendezvous, the village underwent a strong decade of growth in the 1980s. It is located in beautiful coastal Provence about 49 kilometres (30 miles) from Marseille. Sanary has a beautiful coastline with small beaches and is probably the sunniest place in France, with an average of 61 days of rain (mostly in winter) in a year.

We began our visit at the harbour lined with pretty pastels coloured houses.

By the harbour side is a square with a 13th-century medieval watchtower. I was informed that the world-renowned diver Jacques Cousteau (who had visited Sipadan Island) started and developed his diving skills in the waters of Sanary-sur-Mer.

Agape... the most significant word in our lives.

Berthed at the port of Sanary-sur-Mer is a large collection of traditional wooden fishing boats known as *pointus*. The local fishermen sell their catch at the harbour side directly to the many nearby restaurants.

Église Saint Nazaire de Sanary-sur-Mer, a 16th-century church (renovated in the 19th century in a neo-Medieval style). It is located on the main square in the port in the heart of Sanary.

The interior of the church contains beautiful paintings by Jean-Baptiste Garrigou.

Barcelona is the capital city of the autonomous community of Catalonia, Spain, and the country's second largest city. So much is known about Barcelona that it needs no further introduction. Although I had been blessed with many visits to this great city and was no longer a stranger here, I continued to enjoy a walk down La Rambla, even though it was drizzling when we arrived. We spent time a long time at McDonald's, making good use of their complimentary Wi-Fi. Thesw photos here were taken on my previous visits. Wikipedia notes that "Barcelona is one of the world's leading tourist, economic, trade fair, and cultural centres, and its influence in commerce, education, entertainment, media, fashion, science, and the arts all contribute to its status as one of the world's major global cities."

The giant Sagrada Familia basilica, a Gaudí work admired by architects around the world for being one of the most unique and distinctive basilicas.

Park Güell is one of Gaudí artistic works commissioned by Eusebi Güell.

At the top of Park Güell is a terraced area tiled in vibrant colours where you can get a wonderful view of the park and of the city of Barcelona.

Palma de Mallorca is a seaport geographically located in the southwest of Majorca in southern Spain. It is the capital city of the autonomous community of the Balearic Islands. Over the course of its history, the privileged geographical location of the city allowed it to keep extensive commerce with Catalonia and Valencia in Spain, Provence in France, the Maghreb, and Italy, which heralded in the golden age for the city. Since the 1950s, the advent and boom in tourism has caused Palma to grow significantly, transforming it into a centre of attraction for visitors and also attracting workers from mainland Spain. This contributed to a huge change in the traditions and the sociolinguistic map that we noticed today as we strolled along it streets and boulevards.

Palacio Real de la Almudaina (Royal Palace of la Almudaina) with "La Seu" Cathedral of Palma. The Palacio Real de la Almudaina was built in 1309 over an earlier castle.

"La Seu" Cathedral of Palma, designed in the Catalan Gothic style with Northern European influences. King James I of Aragon began the construction in 1229, but it was finished only in 1601.

Now lined with a selection of mid- and high-range shops, the promenade Passeig des Born has been the heart of city life in Palma de Mallorca for over a century. There is also a post box by the corner of the shops (middle of the photo) where you may drop off your postcards.

One of the beautiful fountains of Palma de Mallorca.

Tenerife is the largest island of the seven Canary Islands and is also the largest and most populous island of the whole of Macaronesia. It is a rugged and volcanic island sculpted by successive eruptions throughout its history. As can be seen from the photographs, the uneven and steep orography of the island has resulted in a diversity of landscapes and geographical and geological formations. Christopher Columbus passed from the Canary Islands to the West Indies in 1493. In 1492, he anchored in the Port of Las Palmas (and spent some time on the island) on his first trip to the Americas.

With Santa Cruz de Tenerife, Las Palmas is jointly the capital of the autonomous community of the Canary Islands. Today, about 5 million tourists visit Tenerife each year, the most of any of all the Canary Islands.

A distant view of Santa Cruz de Tenerife.

Panoramic view of the Port of Santa Cruz de Tenerife.

Plaza de España (Spain Square) is the largest square in the city of Santa Cruz de Tenerife. The square is located in the centre of town, just metres north of the Auditorio de Tenerife. It is in the heart of the city with a great artificial lake.

A stroll around the streets of Santa Cruz de Tenerife offers a fascinating experience and a glimpse of its outstanding heritage.

Downtown Santa Cruz de Tenerife. On the right of this photo is the McDonald's. On the left of the photo, opposite the McDonald's, there is a small hotel with open free Wi-Fi in its lobby (just so you know).

On 8 November 2014, the day we were on shore in Tenerife (read the caption of the preceding photo), I updated my family and friends with this Facebook post:

> Provence or Tuscany for retirement? It is not an easy decision for one to make. As a professional homeless person I have recently left (but not forsaken) both... For now I am contented to be a pilgrim/mariner sailing to the New World and hoping to reach land a little easier and faster than Christopher Columbus. The journey continues...

So from the Port of Santa Cruz de Tenerife Canaries, I set sail as a pilgrim/mariner on my voyage across the Atlantic to the eastern shore of the North American continent.

On the early morning of 16 November 2014, having sailed in the open sea from the Canaries in great comfort and for just short seven days, I arrived at the New World. It had taken Columbus (on his first voyage) 33 laborious days and tiresome nights to reach only the East Indies. Change is good.

Eastern coast of the North American continent (Fort Lauderdale, Florida).

Now I stood on solid ground. Well, maybe not so solid in this part of Florida, but it is land on the great American continent. My journey will now continue on land by rail. It has always been my dream to cross the continent by train. I have been told that my paternal great-grandfather and his family (which included my paternal grandfather, who was born in the then-British Guyana) took the train from Halifax across Canada to Vancouver. They were making their way back to China (by boat via Trinidad to Halifax) from British Guyana in South America, where they had spent a number of years in the late 1800s and early 1900s.

Perhaps one day I will (by rail) replicate their journey across Canada from Halifax to Vancouver. But for the present, I was happy to be able to travel across the USA by Amtrak from Fort Lauderdale to Portland, Oregon, and to visualize life in the bygone era of the Transcontinental Railroad (a contiguous rail network that crosses the American landmass). I read somewhere that the Transcontinental Railroad was opened for through-traffic in 1869 with the ceremonial driving of the "Last Spike" at Promontory Summit, barely 100 years prior to Neil Armstrong's 1969 "one small step for [a] man, one giant leap for mankind".

Amtrak Station in Fort Lauderdale.

Silver Meteor from Fort Lauderdale to Washington DC.

So several months ago, I planned and made reservation for this Empire Builder train route across the great continent. This journey would take May and me from Fort Lauderdale to Washington, DC, overnight with the Silver Meteor's comfortable, reclinable reserved coach seats. We would then have an eight-hour transit time in Washington, DC.

From Washington, DC, we took the Capitol Limited to Chicago one night in a Superliner roomette and were delayed for almost five hours because of the previous day's heavy snowstorm, rail upgrade construction, and the freight trains. The freight trains have priority of the rail system. Our transit time in Chicago, originally scheduled for seven hours, was reduced to two because of the delay. From Chicago, we took the Empire Builder for Portland, Oregon, spending two more nights also in a Superliner roomette.

Superliner roomette (Photo courtesy of Amtrak). Not for an oversized person. Needs a wee bit of getting used to. I was fine from the second night on. There is a harness/safety net for the upper bunk.

Relaxing in the day... wishing Amtrak had Wi-Fi from Fort Lauderdale to Portland. There is open free Wi-Fi on board only from Portland to Vancouver, British Columbia.

The price of progress?

A view from Fort Lauderdale to Washington, DC.

Life would be hard for us all without these.

Winter came early this year for this part of the continent.

We do need to replenish the water!

Got the feeling like in The Road to Oregon: *A Chronicle of the Great Emigrant Trail* (1929)?

As they say, "Chill out and watch amazing scenery go by in the Observation Cars."

In retrospect, it is interesting now for me to realize that at the time when I was at Tenerife, somehow I imagined myself as a pilgrim/mariner sailing to the New World. As I boarded the train to take this journey across the great North American continent, I recalled the story I had read so many years ago now about the ship the *Mayflower*, which transported migrants (collectively known today as the "Pilgrims") from the port of Plymouth in England to Virginia in the New World. On the train from Chicago to Portland, we crossed paths with Cloyce, who is a direct descendant of one of the Pilgrim Fathers on the *Mayflower*, and his wife, Alyce, who is a descendant of Sir William Wallace (1270–1305), one of the leaders during the Wars of the Scottish Independence depicted in the movie *Braveheart*, a 1995 epic historical war drama film directed by and starring Mel Gibson.

So Cloyce and Alyce came into our lives unexpectedly and perhaps for a reason. You can imagine the stories we shared with each other on this journey. We felt so blessed.

May with Cloyce and Alyce at the Minot Station in North Dakota.

This is the ending of this story. But this story is not finished...

DID YOU SCROLL ALL THE WAY DOWN HERE FIRST? And do you play cards (Spades, Hearts, Clubs, and Diamonds)?

This trip is a home journey for me—in actuality, not a journey to the New World. It was a "pilgrimage". This home journey also got me questioning what really is the fourth Road that Father Jordi mentioned in *The Pilgrimage* by Paulo Coelho.

Here are the four Roads:

1. The Camino de Santiago, which is the Road of the Spades that will transform our lives if we are willing

2. The Road to Jerusalem, which is the Road to the Hearts or the Road of the Grails; it can endow us with the ability to have revelation of what is unseen, to have visions, and to perform miracles

3. The Road to Rome, which is the Road of the Clubs that allows us to communicate with others and other worlds

4. The Road of the Diamond; Father Jordi never mentioned what the Road of the Diamond is

Just a thought: Perhaps "Diamond" stands for wealth. Real wealth is in the value as we live and share in our "Mundus Novus". Will the Road of the Diamond lead us there? I have come to the realization that the busyness of live had spun me outward from the centre. I am grateful to have stumbled upon the Road of the Diamond—my pilgrim path. This Road may still have ups and downs, but I believe the waymarks are clear and the destination, set. The only thing unsure is when I will arrive.

Peace be with you,

Nicholas

Come walk with me. My journey continues...

New Life (to Be Born Again)

On 4 February 2015, the Sheep Year arrives, which marks the end of the Year of the Horse. This day is not the Chinese New Year Day. It is the day of the start of spring in the Chinese Astrology Calendar. The start of spring in China is noon on 4 February 2015 (20:00 PST on 3 February 2015), the time when the sun enters the 315th degree on the tropical zodiac. I am given to understand that a baby born on 4 February 2015 is a Sheep baby. A new life...

On 4 February 2015, it would have been 100 days since I left the area called "West Bank" or "Israeli-occupied territories"—one of the most "disputed territories" in the world, within which we were attacked (our coach, stoned) and others were killed. I wonder why 100 days is so significant and important in our lives: American presidents first 100 days, Canada's 100 days, Napoleon's 100 days, Grieving Etiquette of 100 days. One hundred days, and yet (for many of us) the smell lingers on... smell of pride, smell of hate, smell of human conflicts, smell of fear, and the smell of death.

The smell of pride, the smell of hate, the smell of human conflicts, the smell of fear, and the smell of death.

The last 100 days have given me the time to reflect—to reflect on the scent of freshness, the scent of love, the scent of joy, and the scent of peace—and to have hope: hope in the Word made flesh.

The scent of freshness, the scent of a new life, the scent of love, the scent of joy, and the scent of peace.

Hope in the Word made flesh.

TO NAZARETH, VILLAGE OF MARY AND THE SITE OF THE ANNUNCIATION...

On our way to the Church of the Annunciation in Nazareth.

On 4 February 2015, it would be 100 days since we left East Jerusalem and sailed from Ashdod to Haifa. From there, we boarded a coach for our journey to the town of Nazareth and to the region around the Sea of Galilee. We visited the Church of the Annunciation in Nazareth, a minor basilica which stands over the cave of the home of the Virgin Mary. The current church is a two-story building constructed in the '60s (completed only in 1969) over the site of earlier churches built in the Byzantine period and during the time of the Crusades.

Outside the church are the cloisters with large mosaics on the walls. The mosaics were donated by various countries or organisations around the world. This church building comprises the oldest part of the existing grotto, where the angel Gabriel appeared before the Virgin Mary. The Grotto of the Annunciation is believed to be the remains of the original childhood home of Mary.

The entrance of the Church of the Annunciation.

The collections of mosaics donated by various countries or organisations around the world.

The upper part of the church.

The upper part of the church is spectacularly constructed with large mosaics on the walls. Though it was relatively crowded at the time of our visit, I was still able to feel the serenity inside. Photographs were taken with reverence. I gazed in awe at the beautiful stained-glass windows and huge, fabulous mosaics on the walls. I was mesmerized.

We then descended to visit the grotto where Mary's house was located. I tried to imagine what would have gone through the mind of young Mary when Gabriel appeared to her with that message, which has changed and transformed the lives of so many. This was where the angel Gabriel revealed to the Virgin Mary that she would conceive and give birth to a son.

Pilgrims/visitors queuing to view the remains of the home of Mary.

Grotto of the Annunciation, believed by many Christians to be the remains of the original childhood home of Mary.

The lower church centres on the Grotto, where we could see remains of the Byzantine and Crusader churches that preceded the current church.

TO THE REGION AROUND THE SEA OF GALILEE...

The Mount of the Beatitudes.

We also had the opportunity to visit the Galilee region, where Jesus grew up as a child and was later baptised and where he began his ministry. The three canonical (synoptic) Gospels of Matthew, Mark, and Luke give account of Jesus's public ministry in this region, particularly in the towns of Nazareth and Capernaum. Galilee is also cited as the place where Jesus performed many public miracles.

Capernaum, which was built along the edge of the Sea of Galilee, was in existence from the 2nd century BC to the 7th century AD.

Jesus makes his home in Capernaum (Matthew 4:12–17). Jesus teaches in the synagogue (Mark 1:21–28). Jesus cures Peter's mother-in-law (Mark 1:29–31). Paying the temple tax (Matthew 17:24–27). Jesus calls Matthew (Matthew 9:9–12. Jesus condemns Capernaum (Matthew 11:20–24). Jesus heals a centurion's servant (Luke 7:1–10). Jesus cures a paralysed man (Mark 2:1–12). "I am the bread of life" (John 6:22–59.

Capernaum synagogue. This partly reconstructed synagogue is believed to have been built on the foundations of the synagogue in which Jesus taught. Erected in the 4th or 5th century, this impressive structure with ornately carved decorations is the largest synagogue discovered in Israel.

Matthew 16:18: "And I say also unto thee, That thou art Peter, and upon this rock I will build my church; and the gates of hell shall not prevail against it."

Two miles west of Capernaum is what Josephus the historian referred to as the "well of Capernaum". Heptapegon (corrupted to "Tabgha"), a popular fishing spot because of its famous "seven springs", is traditionally believed to be the location for several episodes in Jesus's ministry. It is an area situated on the north-western shore of the Sea of Galilee in Israel.

A distant view of the Sea of Galilee in present time.

It is believed that here Jesus walked along the shore and called out to Simon Peter and Andrew, who were casting their fishing nets. Walking along the shore, Jesus also saw two brothers—James (James the Greater—the patron saint of Spain and of the Camino de Santiago) and John (the author of the Gospel of John, three epistles, and the Book of Revelation)—who were preparing their nets with their father Zebedee. Jesus called all of these men to follow him.

"And Jesus said unto them, Come ye after me, and I will make you to become fishers of men" (Mark 1:17).

In this region, we had the opportunity to visit the Church of the Beatitudes, located on a small hill overlooking the Sea of Galilee. The church is built on the site traditionally believed to be where Jesus delivered the Sermon on the Mount. With the quiet, lush gardens overlooking the Sea of Galilee, it is an excellent environment for us to contemplate some of the well-known teachings of Jesus (Matthew 5–7).

The Church of the Beatitudes located by the Sea of Galilee near Tabgha and Capernaum in Israel.

Inside the Church of the Beatitudes. Designed by the architect A. Barluzzi, this Catholic church on the Mount of the Beatitudes is Byzantine in style. Its octagonal shape represents the eight beatitudes.

The Church of the Multiplication.

The interior of the church has a central nave and two aisles. The sanctuary is backed by an apse with transepts on either side. Under the altar is a block of limestone found during excavation; it is venerated as the stone on which the miraculous meal was laid.

The lush and quiet garden of the Church of the Beatitudes.

Pilgrims are known to have commemorated this site since at least the 4th century. A pilgrim named Egeria (circa AD 381) wrote the following in her itinerary of the Holy Land:

> And this is the field where the Lord fed the people with the five loaves and two fishes. In fact the stone on which the Lord placed the bread has now been made into an altar... Past the walls of this church goes the public highway on which the Apostle Matthew had his place of custom. Near there on a mountain is a cave to which the Savior climbed and spoke the Beatitudes.

A NEW LIFE (TO BE BORN AGAIN)

The Jordan River (sometimes referred to as River Jordan) is significant in Judaism, Islam, and Christianity. Immersion in a natural water source—like a river—was and still is a primary Jewish *mitzvah* (commandment).

On this journey to Jerusalem, we crossed paths with a Jewish lady from Melbourne, Australia, and dined with her in the Oceanview Cafe on the *Celebrity Silhouette* cruise ship. She enlightened and told us that she had come to Jerusalem to attend her nephew's Bar Mitzvah and to visit many of the sites holy to her faith. I was given to understand that even in the present time, the tradition regarding the construction of a *mikveh* (bath) are based on the classical rabbinical literature. According to these rules, a *mikveh* must be connected to water from a spring, and thus the water can be supplied by rivers and lakes that have natural springs as their source. Jewish friends whom I met many years ago had also mentioned that the tradition appeared in the famous Dead Sea Scrolls of Qumran.

Portion of the Temple Scroll, which is one of the longest of the Dead Sea Scrolls.

A Muslim by the name of Saba A. from Afghanistan, who reminded me of those two Muslims who took me to St. Peter's Cave Church in Antakya (see the earlier post "Steps of Paul"), has written this review of the River Jordan:

> As a Muslim, we believe in Jesus Christ and respect him greatly, so when I was in Jordan, I knew that I had to visit Christ's Baptismal site... Despite not being a Christian myself, I felt this strange spiritual feeling inside during the entire time I was there. This is definitely the place to go to when in Jordan, since it can easily be done in a day from Amman, and is very close to the Dead Sea as well.

The River Jordan holds a special place in Christianity and in the hearts of many Christians. It is where most modern scholars and archaeologists believe the baptism of Jesus took place, corresponding with the directions given in Matthew 3:13–17, Mark 1:9–11, and Luke 3:21. Many believe there is enormous theological significance in the baptism of Jesus (though he was sinless). It affirmed Jesus as the Messiah of whom John spoke. Jesus revealed the human nature of the Son of God. Jesus is the power for good. He provided an example for all to follow. His baptism displayed a beautiful picture of the Holy Trinity.

The Yardenit Baptismal Site located south of the River Jordan's outlet from the Sea of Galilee.

The Yardenit Baptismal Site frequented by Christian pilgrims is a baptism site located along the River Jordan in the Galilee region of northern Israel. The site is located south of the river's outlet from the Sea of Galilee. The actual site where Jesus was baptized is believed to be in Al-Maghtas, on the Jordan side of the Jordan River.

This Al-Maghtar site is one of the most important recent discoveries in biblical archaeology. Following the peace treaty between Jordan and Israel in 1994, excavations at Al-Maghtas started in 1996 and have already uncovered more than 20 churches, caves, and baptismal pools dating from the Roman and Byzantine periods. Although the identification is not absolutely certain, archaeology has shown that the area known as Wadi Kharrar has long been believed to be the biblical Bethany-beyond-the-Jordan, where John the Baptist lived and Jesus was baptized.

The River Jordan today. Mark 1:9–11 (*English Standard Version*): "In those days Jesus came from Nazareth of Galilee and was baptized by John in the Jordan. And when he came up out of the water, immediately he saw the heavens being torn open and the Spirit descending on him like a dove. And a voice came from heaven, 'You are my beloved Son; with you I am well pleased.'"

Over the centuries and down through the ages, this modest river has assumed importance significant mythical proportions for many Christians. It was in River Jordan that Jesus came to be baptized—a moment that marked the beginning of his ministry. The baptismal site of Yardenit welcomes over half a million pilgrims/visitors annually who come to experience the spirituality and imbuing power of the waters of River Jordan.

Baptism in River Jordan is being carried out at the Yardenit Baptismal Site, located along the River Jordan in the Galilee region of northern Israel.

As I tried to touch my forehead with the water from River Jordan, I saw the reflection of myself in the river. I recalled the Greek mythology that I read a long time ago about Narcissus and wondered in that fleeting moment whether I had really been reborn...

PILGRIM

Peace be with you,

Nicholas

Just a thought: On this, my journey, I once again touch the water in renewal. As I look past my own reflection, I see a world beyond—a world of peace. There is hope in the Prince of Peace... hope in the Word made flesh.

My journey continues. Come walk with me...

The Way (Spiritual Space)

"If interreligious dialogue is to bear fruit—the fruit of mutual understanding, respect, and peace—it needs to be rooted in the specific spiritual space or milieu of each religious tradition. If we are willing to enter into and even dwell for a time in another spiritual space, we will be able to return to the space we call home, enriched by the gifts we have received and prepared to live in peace with those who dwell in a spiritual space that is very different from our own."

—Benoit Standaert (Benedictine monk at St. Andrew's Abbey in Bruges, Belgium)

The Shwedagon Pagoda.

The Second Vatican Council, in its *Declaration on the Relation of the Church to Non-Christian Religions*, said, "The Church rejects nothing that is true and holy in these religions." I have sought to ground my faith by allying Christianity with mysticism. With the gift of wisdom coming from and arising out of this mystical experience of nonduality, I hope Christianity would return to being (for me) an even more inwardly directed religion.

On 21 March 2015, I arrived Thilawa (Rangoon), Myanmar. *Myanmar* (also called *Burma* by the British) is the name used by its people for their homeland. King Anawrahta formed the country in the 11th century. Due to the invasion of the Mongols, the empire collapsed 200 years later. The city of Yangon was only founded in 1755. By 1852, the British had seized Burma, transforming Yangon into a prosperous trading centre and anglicising the name to *Rangoon*.

I first heard of this name as a little child, when my parents went there on leave under the aegis of Harrisons & Crosfield. The name *Rangoon* has stuck in my mind ever since. I have always dreamed of making a cultural pilgrimage to this mystical land. So I arrived Thilawa (Rangoon) more than 60 years after my dad had first visited it. Upon arrival in Myanmar, I took a coach to visit two of the most significant sites in Yangon and Bago.

A view of the Bago River.

Bago is located on the eastern bank of the Bago River in Lower Myanmar and was founded in AD 825 by the Mons, who migrated from China. King Binya U established his palace in Bago in the 14th century, and it became the ancient capital city of the Mon Kingdom in the 15th century, when it was known as Pegu.

My visit to Myanmar would be incomplete without a journey to visit the Shwedagon Pagoda in Yangon and the Shwethalyaung Buddha, which is a reclining Buddha on the west side of Bago. I eventually noticed that aspects of Burmese culture are most apparent in religious sites. The country has been called the "Land of Pagodas" because the landscape is dominated by Buddhist pagodas or stupas (in various states of repair), which have stood for nearly a millennium.

According to legend, the Shwedagon was constructed more than 2,600 years ago, making it the oldest Buddhist stupa in the world. Archaeologists and historians, however, maintain that the pagoda was built by the Mon between 6th and 10th centuries AD ("The Shwedagon Pagoda." *Journal of the Burma Research Society*: 1–91). The Shwedagon Pagoda is located on the 114-acre Singuttara Hill, west of the Royal Lake in Yangon. It is the most sacred and impressive Buddhist site for the people of Myanmar.

A view of the landscape from the Sanguttara Hill in Dagon Township, Yangon Division.

To the Shwedagon Pagoda.

Entrance to the site.

In various stages of repair.

Visitors are required to remove shoes before entering the site as a mark of respect.

Even though I grew up in multicultural Malaysia, where I still have many Buddhist (Mahayana) friends, this journey would still grant me a better understanding and an insider's view of the magnificent symbol of Theravada Buddhism in the lives of the Myanmar people. I realize that the Shwedagon forms the focus of religious as well as the community activities of the people of Myanmar.

Religious procession.

Religious/community life.

Procession for a family member joining the monastic life.

Many of the practices of the monkhood are clearly understood only by those who are born into traditional Buddhist cultures.

With " humility and reverence". This is the monastic way, not unlike the Benedictine way in the tradition of Christianity. However, in Christianity (unlike New Age spirituality), there is no "losing of individuality" because to me the ultimate goal of contemplative prayer is to beunited with Christ.

On this day, I visited the Shwedagon twice—I was determined to see this place once more in its splendour at night. The pagoda stands 110 metres and is covered with hundreds of gold plates. The site is indeed a repository of Myanmar heritage, including architecture, sculpture, and other art.

PILGRIM

The spectacular pagoda at sunset.

Visitors are offered an opportunity to light up the site.

Lighting up the site.

Witnessing the hitting of the gong.

One of the images of Buddha.

Hitting the gong (I generated the loudest sound among the gongmen)!

During my journey to this mystical land, I also had the opportunity to visit the Shwethalyaung Buddha, which is a reclining Buddha in the west side of Bago (Pegu). The Buddha, which is 55 metres (180 feet) long with a height of 16 metres (52 feet), is the second largest Buddha in the world (after the 74-metre reclining Buddha in Dawei, Myanmar). The Buddha is believed to have been built during the reign of Mon King in in AD 994. It was believed to be lost in the 18th century when Bago was pillaged. When Britain occupied Burma after the second Anglo-Burmese War, the Shwethalyaung Pagoda was rediscovered under the jungle growth. Restoration of the Shwethalyaung began in 1881, and Buddha's mosaic pillows (on its left side) were added in 1930.

On the way to visit the Shwethalyaung Buddha.

The Shwethalyaung Buddha.

The Buddha is 55 metres long with a height of 16 metres.

For scale purposes only.

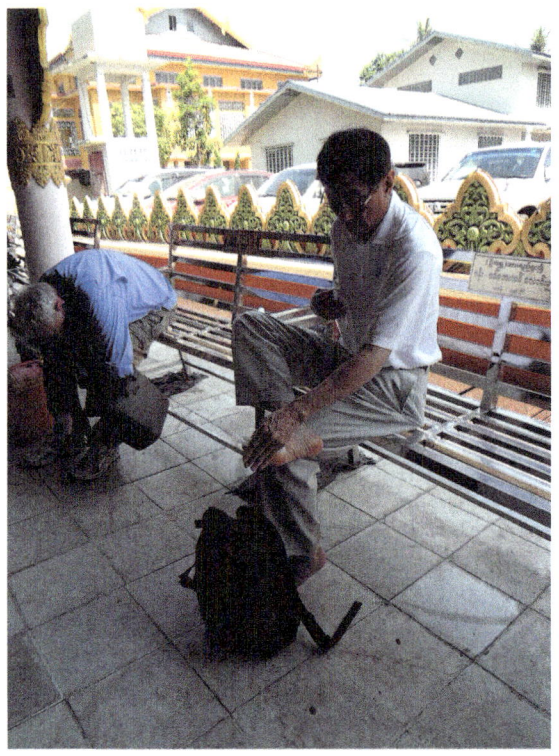

Self-explanatory.

Myanmar is predominantly a Theravada Buddhist country. According to its own accounts, the Theravada school is fundamentally derived from the "doctrine of analysis".

Images of Buddha.

The name *Theravada* comes from the ancestral Sthavira, from which the Theravadins claim descent. A group broke away from the Mahāsāṃghikas during the Second Buddhist Council, giving rise to the Sthavira sect. Theravada accounts its own origins to the teachings (known as the Vibhajjavāda) agreed upon during the putative Third Buddhist Council under the patronage of the Indian Emperor Ashoka (250 BC). The Vibhajjavādins in turn is said to have split into four groups: the Mahīśāsaka, Kāśyapīya Dharmaguptaka, and Tāmraparnīya.

Theravada is a branch of Buddhism that uses the teaching of the Pāli Canon (a collection of the oldest recorded Buddhist texts) as its doctrinal core but also includes a rich diversity of traditions and practices that have developed over its long history of interactions with various cultures and communities. In recent times, Theravada Buddhism has taken root in the West and in the Buddhist revival in India. Theravada Buddhists, otherwise known as Theravadins, are believed to number over 150 million worldwide. The Theravada sect appears to be more orthodox, while the Mahāyāna and some other sects tend to be more liberal in their outlook and religious observances.

In spite of changing circumstances and environments, the Theravada sect tried to observe the Vinaya to the very letter. Even though minor changes to the precepts had taken place from time to time (for example, the rule regarding the partaking of food after the stipulated time of the day), the changes were not officially recognized. The Theravada sect has not openly acknowledged the fact that certain variations can be allowed under special circumstances. Some monks insist on observing the very letter of the Vinaya code rather than its spirit. The Theravada sect has continued to adhere to the use of the original robes that were traditionally prescribed, despite the changed social and climatic conditions.

Mahayana is the Buddhism practised in China, Indonesia, Malaysia, Vietnam, Korea, Tibet, and Japan. It constitutes an inclusive tradition characterized by plurality and the adoption of new Mahayana sutras in addition to the earlier Āgama texts. Mahayana sees itself as penetrating further and more profoundly into the Buddha's Dharma with expansive doctrines. There is also a tendency in Mahayana sutras to regard adherence to these sutras as generating spiritual benefits greater than those that arise from being a follower of the non-Mahayana approaches to Dharma.

The fundamental principles of Mahayana doctrine were based on the possibility of universal liberation from suffering for all beings (hence, the "Great Vehicle") and the existence of Buddhas and bodhisattvas (enlightened individuals) embodying Buddha Nature.

The Pure Land school of Mahayana simplifies the expression of faith by allowing salvation to be alternatively obtained through the grace of the Amitābha Buddha by having faith and devoting oneself to the mindfulness of Buddha. This devotional lifestyle of Buddhism has greatly contributed to the success of Mahayana in East Asia, where spiritual elements have traditionally relied upon mindfulness of the Buddha and the reading of Mahayana sutras. In Chinese Buddhism, most monks, let alone lay people, practise Pure Land, with some people combining it with Chan (Zen).

Chan-Thar-Gyi Buddha image.

Most Mahayana schools believe in supernatural bodhisattvas who devote themselves to the perfection, ultimate knowledge, and the liberation of all sentient beings. In Mahayana, the Buddha is seen as the ultimate highest being present in all times in all beings and in all places, and the bodhisattvas come to represent the universal ideal of altruistic excellence.

Instruction in Theravada Buddhism.

Buddhists nowadays are still concerned with the special rules given by the founder of Buddhism, as shown at the International Congress on Buddhist Women's Role in the Sangha held at the University of Hamburg, Germany, in 2007. Female monastics are known as bhikkhunīs.

The Sthavira from which Theravada is derived differs from other early Buddhist schools on a variety of teachings. The differences resulted from the systemisation of the Buddhist teachings, which was preserved in the Abhidhammas of the various schools. The Abhidhamma is a restatement of the doctrine of the Buddha in strictly formalised language, assumed to constitute a consistent system of philosophy. Its aim is not the empirical verification of the Buddhist teachings but "to set forth the correct interpretation of the Buddha's statements in the Sutra to restate his 'system' with perfect accuracy".

The use of *mantra*, or the repetition of certain phrases, in Pāli is an extremely common form of meditation in the Theravada tradition.

In Theravada Buddhism, one of the main spiritual elements of sangha is to come together for meditation and prayer.

Burmese female devotees pour water over an image of the Buddha at the Shwedagon Pagoda in Rangoon. This ritual is seen as a way of paying respect to the person of the Buddha himself.

Novice monks.

Buddhism reached Burma around the beginning of the Christian era, mingling with Hinduism (also imported from India) and indigenous animism.

Christianity was brought to Burma by European missionaries in the 1800s. It made little if any headway among Buddhists but has been widely adopted by non-Buddhists such as the Chin Karen and Kachin. The Roman Catholic School and Myanmar Baptist Convention are the largest Christian denominations in Burma. After the United States, Burma is home to the second largest population of Baptists in the world.

At the age of 25, Adoniram Judson (9 August 1788–12 April 1850) became the first Protestant missionary sent from North America to preach in Burma. He was an American Baptist missionary who served in Burma for almost 40 years. American Baptist missionary couple Arthur Carson (1860–1908) and his wife, Laura (1858–1942), arrived in Burma on 15 March 1899 and opened a mission station in

Hakha in Chin State. Later, other missionaries joined them and did extensive mission works throughout the Chin Hills and converted most of the Northern Chin State to Christianity within a century. This missionary work brought education, development, social, and economic changes and health improvement to the Chin people. Christians were persecuted after the military takeover of Burma in the 1960s.

Approximately 4–6 percent of the population of Myanmar are Christians today.

Peace be with you,

Nicholas

Just a thought: In another age and time and in other culture, it might be different. In the First World (in this age and time), very few enter the monastery just because it is there. Some enter not because society points them there but because somehow they sense that they will find God inside. As someone not called to live a monastic life, I need to find myself grounded in the idea that God's presence is everywhere. It is incumbent upon me to seek this out as follower of Christ and live life in a holistic manner with a constant reminder of the reality of the Incarnation.

For me, Jesus is the Way: "Jesus saith unto him, I am the way, the truth, and the life: no man cometh unto the Father, but by me" (John 14:6, KJV). But what are the "many mansions"?

John 14:2 (KJV) says, "In my Father's house are many mansions; if it were not so, I would have told you. I go to prepare a place for you." Perhaps "by him", there is hope for everyone (willing) to find a place in the Kingdom of God... even for the unbaptised (for those who had come before John the Baptist, for the one who repented and died on the cross next to our Saviour, and for those who will come after and are willing to follow His Way (the Path to His Kingdom).

> "For I do not seek to understand in order to believe, but I believe in order to understand. For I believe this: unless I believe, I will not understand."
>
> —Anselm of Canterbury
> *My journey continues...*

Clash of Cultures

As we sailed in the Baltic Sea towards St. Petersburg, a beautiful rainbow appeared in the sky. It reminded me of Genesis 9:17: "And God said unto Noah, This is the token of the covenant, which I have established between me and all flesh that is upon the earth."

Rainbow appearing in the Baltic Sea.

Equestrian monument to Nicholas I at Isaakievskaya Ploshchad (St. Isaac's Square) in St. Petersburg, Russia.

Friday, 26 June 2015—St. Petersburg.

Our Captain's Log: As we approach the pilot station this morning, we completed our steering and engines checks, ringing standby engines at 0315. At 0325 with our pilot on board, we proceeded through the St. Petersburg Dam, passing Kotlin Island and the city of Kronstadt on our port side at 0407. Under the direction of the pilot, we followed the narrow channel towards St. Petersburg. At 0540 we made a tug fast aft, which helped us manoeuvre into position alongside our berth in the city. We were all fast by 0645 and ready to commence passenger operations.

Approaching St. Petersburg.

On this very day as we arrived St. Petersburg, a deeply divided Supreme Court of the United States (SCOTUS) delivered a historic victory to the gay rights movement, ruling five-to-four that same-sex couples be allowed to marry nationwide. The White House was bathed in rainbow colours to celebrate the Supreme Court's decision... and the same rainbow colours appeared before us in the Baltic on the other side of the world. The White House issued the following statement:

> Tonight, the White House was lit to demonstrate our unwavering commitment to progress and equality, here in America and around the world. The pride colors reflect the diversity of the LGBT community, and tonight, these colors celebrate a new chapter in the history of American civil rights.

It is not of my choosing, but it is incumbent upon me to write about this in "Clash of Cultures". Not so long ago (when we still believed in the Scriptures), my American friends used to say to me,

"Love the sinner, hate the sin." However, our position on this marriage issue (including that of the incumbent American president and at least one aspiring 2016 presidential candidate) has evolved at warp speed over the last few years. I know that some of my gay relatives and friends still do not believe in nor do they support same-sex marriage, but many in the secular world do. We quote, *"Tempora mutantur, nos et mutamur in illis"* (Times change, and we change with them), even though we know that truth is constant!

Truth never evolves! Why, then, has our view evolved suddenly? So what was on my mind after SCOTUS handed down its 5–4 decision? I posted on my Facebook wall: "Did the majority in SCOTUS fall short in discernment by granting ostensible right to self-serving individuals against the interests of the community thereby driving the final nail into the coffin of common good?" I posted this because I believe same-sex marriage is not for the common good. I believe and understand that the Paraclete (Holy Spirit) intercedes only for the common good.

On the other side of the world (in a different culture), the real rainbow came out for us. As we journeyed towards St. Petersburg, we received the following important notification: *New Russian Law.*

Russia has recently enacted a law prohibiting certain type of behavior including waving rainbow flags, pride parades and conspicuous displays of same sex affection. Possible punishment include jail time and expulsion from the country. It is unclear how this law will be enforced, but we urge our guests to avoid any behavior that might run afoul of this law.

I do not understand why (by "coincidence"?) I was notified of this Russian law on the very day SCOTUS (with ostensible authority) "legislated" the complete opposite. I have journeyed into and experienced in a profound way many other different cultures, traditions, and beliefs. I know that we do not call others "haters" simply because they hold a view different from ours. I took cognizance of this "coincidence". I disembarked, constantly reminding myself that I needed to respect others' cultures and traditions and to obey their laws and regulations (bearing in mind the lessons learned by the Westerners who stripped themselves naked on Mount Kinabalu

Sabah Malaysia). On that occasion on 30 May 2015 without regards and respect for local laws and customs ten Westerners stripped themselves naked at the summit of Mount Kinabalu a mountain long revered as sacred by many locals. Four of them (two Canadian siblings one Dutch citizen and British National) were later arrested before they could leave the country. They were charged for committing obscene act in public and all four pleaded guilty and were each fined Malaysian Ringgits MYR5000 and sentenced to three days in jail.

I would have failed miserably if I had kept quiet and not written about this incident or "coincidence" from our journey to St. Petersburg. Suppressing the news of this incident would be a distortion of the truth of my own struggle.

Modern-day St. Petersburg.

For many years, I have tried to understand Eastern (Greek) Orthodoxy. The Russian Orthodox Church officially ranks fifth in the Orthodox order of precedence, right under the four Greek Patriarchates of the Greek Orthodox Church (those of Constantinople, Alexandria, Antioch, and Jerusalem). The Primate of the Russian Orthodox Church is the Patriarch of Moscow and all Russia.

The Church of the Saviour on Spilled Blood. Architecturally, this cathedral differs from St. Petersburg's other structures. The Saviour on Spilled Blood harks back to medieval Russian architecture, even though the city's architecture is predominantly Baroque and Neoclassical.

I am given to understand that "In the Eastern Orthodox Church, candles are lit before icons, usually of Jesus Christ or the Holy Theotokos. Usually Orthodox churches only use long, thin candles. These are usually placed in round containers, having either various sockets to hold the candles, or in a container filled with sand, in which the worshippers place their candles. Orthodox churches will usually have a separate place to put candles lit for the departed; Anglican and Roman Catholic churches make no such distinction" (Wikipedia, "Votive candle").

Russian Orthodoxy (geopolitical importance of Russia aside) has fascinated me since I learned of the event that occurred on 13 May 1917 in Fatíma, Portugal (refer my blog post "Fatíma"). The story of Fatíma began with the backdrop of the First World War, which involved Europe in some of the most horrific warfare the world had ever known. The year 1917 was also a major turning point in Russian history and also the Russian Orthodox Church. The Russian revolution dismantled the Tsarist autocracy that led to the eventual rise of the Soviet Union.

The Russian Empire collapsed with the abdication of Emperor Nicholas II. The beginning of this civil war would plunge Russia and later Eastern Europe into the oppression of atheistic governments for the next six decades. The Bolsheviks took power in October 1917.

For the first time in its history, the Russian Orthodox Church found itself without official backing of the state. This led to a marked decline in the power and influence of the Church. Many leaders of the Church supported the White Movement, which would ultimately turn out to be the losing side. The Soviet government stood on a platform of anti-religion. It viewed the church as a "counter-revolutionary" organisation and also as an independent voice with tremendous influence in the Russian society. I was given to understand that openly religious people could not join the Communist Party, which meant that they could not hold any political office.

The Church and the government remained on unfriendly terms until 1988. A pivotal point in the history of the Russian Orthodox Church came in 1988—the millennial anniversary of the Baptism of Kievan Rus'. Throughout the summer of that year, major government-supported celebrations took place in Moscow and other cities. Many older churches and some monasteries were reopened. For the first time in the history of the Soviet Union, people could see live transmissions of church services on television.

Another magnificent Orthodox church came into view as we proceeded along Moskovsky Prospekt.

So putting aside politics, I entered St. Petersburg (Russia's "Window on the West") with the same thrill and excitement I had felt at the time I held Tolstoy's *War and Peace* in my hand. St. Petersburg remains (for me) one of the great metropolises. It has provided a historic world stage since the day Peter the Great ordained its construction on the banks of the Neva River. In its relatively short history, St. Petersburg has witnessed the rise and fall of Imperial Russia, three shattering revolutions, and a devastating civil war. It became a symbol of Russian resistance to the Nazi invasion and survived a long and tragic siege during World War II. Perched on the banks of the Neva, the city is crisscrossed by canals. Peter the Great instilled architectural and building ideas in his successors, making the then-capital of Imperial Russia one of the architectural treasures of the world.

Looking at Saint Isaac's Cathedral, or Isaakievskiy Sobor, the largest Russian Orthodox cathedral in St. Petersburg. It is the largest Orthodox basilica and the fourth largest cathedral in the world. The cathedral is a Late Neoclassical rendering of a Byzantine Greek-cross church.

The Rostral Column. The architect of the Old Stock Exchange, Jean-Francois, decided to build the towers in the style of Roman *rostral columns*—victory columns on which the prows ("rostra") of captured enemy ships were mounted.

The Catherine Palace (a Rococo palace) located in the town of Tsarskoye Selo (Pushkin), 25 kilometres southeast of St. Petersburg.

View from the Hermitage Pavilion.

View from the garden (south side).

Inside the Catherine Palace.

Two great architects (Rastrelli and Carlo Rossi) helped bring Peter the Great's vision of St. Petersburg to life. The rich architecture that resulted features a mixture of styles, from ornate Russian Baroque churches to Neoclassical palaces. St. Petersburg to me is without doubt one of the world's most exquisite cities. It has also been the cultural soul of Russia and a home to poets, musicians, and composers ranging from Pushkin to Shostakovich. Although not easily observed, the city is, however, still flanked by meretricious modern design encircled by buildings constructed during the brutal Soviet era.

Life in modern Russia after the brutal Soviet era.

A bridal car.

A limo.

Venetian-inspired canals.

The golden domes and spires of St. Nicholas Cathedral soaring towards the heavens.

However, as I walked along Nevsky Prospekt, catching sight of the city's coloured buildings or watching in awe the golden spires of fairy-tale fortresses and domes of heavenly churches lit by the sunlight, I had the enduring feeling that St. Petersburg is no longer an urban purgatory. Perhaps Russia has already been consecrated? The consecration of Russia to the Immaculate Heart of Mary was reportedly requested by the Virgin Mary on several occasions, beginning in Fatíma, Portugal, in 1917. Ignoring differing political views, do we believe Russia has already been consecrated?

Despite our political views, has Russia already been consecrated?

I believe, however, that "When pride cometh, then cometh shame: but with the lowly is wisdom (Proverbs 11:2, KJV). Biblical cross-references (common denominators) are "Pride goes before destruction, a haughty spirit before a fall" and "Before a downfall the heart is haughty, but humility comes before honour."

As a follower of Christ, I need to be gracious to others and be tolerant of disagreement over disputable matters but discern the truth. I am also instructed that people of faith do not seek to understand in order to believe, but they believe in order to understand; that "the wicked, through the pride of his countenance, will not seek after God: God is not in all his thoughts" (Psalms 10:4, KJV) "and with all deceivableness of unrighteousness in them that perish; because they received not the love of the truth, that they might be saved" (2 Thessalonians 2:10, KJV).

We are to "contend for the faith which was once delivered unto the saints" (Jude 1:3, KJV), "holding fast the faithful word as [we] hath been taught, that [we] may be able by sound doctrine both to exhort and to convince the gainsayers" (Titus 1:9, KJV).

> "Beloved, believe not every spirit, but try the spirits whether they are of God: because many false prophets are gone out into the world."
>
> —1 John 4:1 (KJV)

Resources and Further Reading

Archaeology

Cyber-Archaeology in the Holy Land: The Future of the Past (http://c795631.r31.cf2.rackcdn.com/cyber_archaeology_in_the_holy_land_the_future_of_the_past.pdf)

"Excavations in Ancient Corinth: History and Timeline" (www.ascsa.edu.gr/index.php/excavationcorinth/corinth-history)

"Fathers Virgilio Corbo and Stanislao Loffreda" (www.capernaum.custodia.org/default.asp?id=5380)

"Golgotha: A Reconsideration of the Evidence for the Sites of Jesus' Crucifixion and Burial" (www.biblearchaeology.org/post/2010/01/11/golgotha-a-reconsideration-of-the-evidence-for-the-sites-of-jesuse28099-crucifixion-and-burial.aspx#Article)

Buildings and Other Architecture

"Bayon" (http://en.wikipedia.org/wiki/Bayon)

"Great Hypostyle Hall" (http://en.wikipedia.org/wiki/Great_Hypostyle_Hall)

"Karnak" (http://en.wikipedia.org/wiki/Karnak)

"Ta Prohm" (http://en.wikipedia.org/wiki/Ta_Prohm)

"The Shwedagon Pagoda." *Journal of the Burma Research Society*: 1–91.

"The Western Wall" (http://english.thekotel.org)

Customs and Concepts

"Devotion and Use of the Manna of Saint Nicholas" (www.stnicholascenter.org/pages/manna/)

"Private revelation" (http://en.wikipedia.org/wiki/Private_revelation)

"Sister Lucy States: 'Russia Is Not Yet Properly Consecrated'" (www.fatima.org/weop/e6cp10.asp)

"St. Nicholas, Santa Claus & Father Christmas" (www.whychristmas.com/customs/fatherchristmas.shtml)

"Votive candle" (http://en.wikipedia.org/wiki/Votive_candle)

Historical Events

"Burma's 'forgotten' Chin people suffer abuse" (http://news.bbc.co.uk/2/hi/asia-pacific/8626008.stm)

"The Destruction of Pompeii, 79 AD" (www.eyewitnesstohistory.com/pompeii.htm)

Dynastic Lycia: A Political History of Lycians and Their Relations with Foreign Powers, c. 545–362 B.C., by Anthony G. Keen

"First Crusade" (http://en.wikipedia.org/wiki/First_Crusade)

Paul *Apostle of the Heart Set Free* F.F. Bruce

Organisations

"Catholic Church" (http://en.wikipedia.org/wiki/Catholic_Church)

"Inner Temple" (http://en.wikipedia.org/wiki/Inner_Temple)

"Lourdes Medical Bureau" (http://en.wikipedia.org/wiki/Lourdes_Medical_Bureau)

People

"Jacinta and Franicsco Marto" (http://en.wikipedia.org/wiki/Jacinta_and_Francisco_Marto)

"Lúcia Santos" (http://en.wikipedia.org/wiki/Lúcia_Santos)

"Our Lady of Fatíma" (http://en.wikipedia.org/wiki/Our_Lady_of_Fátima)

Places (Geographical and Political)

Exploring Jordan: The Other Biblical Land (2008, Biblical Archaeology Society).

"Kingdom of Cyprus" (http://en.wikipedia.org/wiki/Kingdom_of_Cyprus)

"Haroun Mountain" (http://nabataea.net/haroun.html)

"Sela: Edom" (http://en.wikipedia.org/wiki/Sela_(Edom))

"West Bank" (http://en.wikipedia.org/wiki/West_Bank)

Travel and Transportation

"Camino Frances or the French Way" (www.followthecamino.com/camino-frances-cat2.html)

Eurail (www.eurail.com)

"Pau Pyrénées Airport" (http://en.wikipedia.org/wiki/Pau_Pyrénées_Airport)

"SCNF" (http://en.wikipedia.org/wiki/SNCF)

"Tarbes–Lourdes–Pyrénées Airport" (http://en.wikipedia.org/wiki/Tarbes–Lourdes–Pyrénées_Airport)

"TGV" (http://en.wikipedia.org/wiki/TGV)

About the Author

Born in 1942 in British North Borneo (Sabah, Malaysia) and now residing in Vancouver, British Columbia, the Nicholas Fung has had an interesting and varied professional life. Trained as a Barrister-at-Law at The Honourable Society of The Inner Temple, he was called to the Bar of England and Wales in 1966. Eventually returning to Sabah, he has served as the State Attorney-General, was the founder and president of The Council of The Justices of The Peace, and a founding member and president of The Sabah Golf and Country Club. He was appointed by The Central Bank Malaysia (Bank Negara) as Chairman and Chief Executive of Sabah Bank, tasked with restructuring the bank (which has since merged with Alliance Bank Malaysia), and it is from this position that he ultimately retired.

That is when his journey truly began. Travelling light, in the constant search for an inner spiritual path, he started exploring the world, sharing and enjoying stories, hoping to counter bigotry with knowledge, and letting people see that peace can be achieved even when there are differences between us.

It is with that dedication that he hopes to inspire others to open a space in their busy secular lives and allow for deep and profound personal transformations.

CPSIA information can be obtained
at www.ICGtesting.com
Printed in the USA
LVOW05*2023120816
500044LV00011B/20/P